W9-AZB-119

ON

THE BUDDHA

Bart Gruzalski
Pacific Center for Sustainable Living

Wadsworth
Thomson Learning

Australia • Canada • Denmark • Japan • Mexico • New Zealand • Philippines
Puerto Rico • Singapore • Spain • United Kingdom • United States

Printed in the United States of America
 2 3 4 5 6 7 03 02 01 00

For permission to use material from this text, contact us:
Web: www.thomsonrights.com
Fax: 1-800-730-2215
Phone: 1-800-730-2214

For more information, contact:
Wadsworth/Thomson Learning
10 Davis Drive
Belmont, CA 94002-3098
USA
www.wadsworth.com

ISBN: 0-534-57596-X

Contents

Preface

In this book we explore the central teachings of the Buddha: the Four Noble Truths, the Eightfold Path, the Buddha's analysis of the self, Buddhist ethics, lovingkindness, compassion, mindfulness, meditation, dependent origination, and alms mendicancy. In studying these topics we are not studying the Buddhist religion, which includes various rituals, cultural traditions, beliefs, and practices. Instead, we are studying what the Buddha taught, an ancient wisdom tradition that monastics and laypersons have used as a path for liberation for more than two thousand five hundred years.

Scholars generally agree that the early Pali texts, now part of the Theravada tradition, are the best historical source for the teachings of the Buddha. We will rely on these Pali texts and their interpretations in the first eight chapters of this book before turning, in the last three chapters, to Mahayana Buddhism, Zen Buddhism, and Vajrayana. In these final three chapters we will explore the idea of emptiness, the Bodhisattva ideal, and the claim of universal Buddha-nature, comparing each of these central Mahayana teachings with what we find in the Pali texts of Theravada Buddhism. Because these later three traditions rest on the basic teachings of the Buddha, the person whose primary interest is in Mahayana, Zen or Vajrayana will find the earlier chapters helpful for understanding Buddhism and its practice.

The Buddha said that all he taught was suffering and the way out of suffering. These teachings are relevant today, for human insecurities and human vulnerability to disappointment, grief, and despair are not fundamentally different from what they were at the time of the Buddha. In addition to their relevance, these teachings are also profoundly philosophical, for the solution to the problem of suffering requires the realization of the nature of phenomena.

The Buddha As Philosopher

The reader with a philosophical bent will notice that the Buddha's teachings are precise and philosophically sophisticated, as the following two examples show. First, the Buddha was an ineffabilist on transcendental issues, and his method for dealing with transcendental questions predated by two thousand five hundred years the methodology recommended by twentieth-century philosopher Ludwig Wittgenstein. Second, the Buddha's style of analysis of the "self," a central teaching of the Buddha, is not found in Western philosophy until the eighteenth century, and this mode of analysis remains at the cutting-edge of contemporary philosophical discussions.[1]

In the philosophy of the Buddha we find no divergence between theory and practice, unlike much of contemporary Western philosophy. The Buddha's teachings always point to what can be experienced. The Buddha neither encouraged nor required a belief in anything transcendental. Instead, he insisted that we begin from where we are and not from a theory, a transcendent reality, or a rational point of view. E.A. Burtt believed that this meant, for the Buddha, taking experience as an unqualifiedly dynamic process. Burtt believed that "the challenge of this idea has by no means been fully appreciated, either by the philosophies of the East or by those of the West."[2]

Terminology and Textual Source Material

The *Triple Basket*, or *Tipitaka*, contain the three collections of the canonical Pali texts of Theravada Buddhism. These collections are: the *Vinaya*, which includes the rules for monks and nuns and some of the Buddha's general teachings; the *Nikayas*, collections of suttas which record the general teachings of the Buddha; and the *Abhidhamma*, a collection of scholastic analyses of aspects of these teachings. Since my aim is to present the basic ideas of the Buddha and to let them speak for themselves, I have restricted my source material to the *Vinaya* and the *Nikayas* (note that both the *Udana* and the *Dhammapada* are part of the *Khuddaka Nikaya*). The one exception is the *Visuddhimagga*, a Pali text that many scholars take to be a canonical interpretation of the basic teachings. I use the classical abbreviations listed on page v in referring to these materials, and I follow standard notation in referring to passages and suttas.[3]

In the first eight chapters I use the anglicization of the Pali words as they are found in the Theravada texts rather than their Sanskrit renditions that are sometimes more common in English but come from Mahayana texts. For example, the Pali 'Gotama' replaces the Sanskrit 'Gautama', the Pali 'Nibbana' replaces 'Nirvana', and 'sutta' replaces 'sutra'. Since the basic texts for the material in the last three chapters are in Sanskrit, I return to the anglicizations of Sanskrit to maintain consistency with source material.

Further Reading

The best sources for further reading are the primary texts themselves. For the primary texts of Mahayana, Zen, and Vajrayana, I refer the reader to the endnotes of each chapter. For secondary material on Theravada, Mahayana, Zen and Vajrayana, I refer the reader to the endnotes.[4]

Since most of this book is about the teachings of the Buddha as they come to us through the Theravada tradition, I list the most accessible translations of the primary texts currently in print in the section entitled "Abbreviations." In addition to the many books cited in the endnotes, another source for further exploration of Theravada material is the Web page, "Access to Insight" [http://world.std.com/~metta], which contains an index, a glossary, translations of some Pali texts, texts of some secondary material, and numerous links to other sites.

----

1. In *Reasons and Persons* (Oxford: Claredon Press, 1984), Derek Parfit claims that the Buddha would have agreed with the Reductionist View (p. 273) and cites the Buddha in support of his claim that it is possible to believe this truth about ourselves (p. 280). Parfit ends the book with a section, "Buddha's View," a short compilation of eight quotations from Buddhist sources (pp. 502-503).

2. E.A. Burtt, "The Contributions of Buddhism to Philosophic Thought," in *Knowledge and Conduct* (Kandy, Ceylon: Buddhist Publication Society, 1963), p. 45.

3. I follow the classical abbreviations for texts, e.g., 'M' for '*Majjhima-nikaya*'. Another style of abbreviation adds 'N' for 'nikaya' and so 'MN' abbreviates '*Majjhima-nikaya*'. When a specific reference begins with a lower-case Roman number, e.g. "iii," I am using the Pali text pagination. When I refer to chapter, section, and/or verse, I begin with upper-case Roman numbers, e.g., "III," or Arabic numbers, e.g., "3."

4. I cite some books that are only distributed free and must be requested from the relevant publisher or monastery. For books by Ajahn Sumedho, Ajahn Sucitto, and P.A. Payutto, please send a donation to cover mailing costs to Amaravati Buddhist Monastery, Great Gaddesden, Hemel Hempstead, Hertfordshire, HP1 3BZ, U.K.

Acknowledgments

This book relied on the support of many people. My thanks go, first, to my spouse, Marion Wilson-Gruzalski, a "noble friend" on the path who also proofread numerous drafts. Next, my thanks go to Ajahn Sumedho, another "noble friend," who has taught me much about the basic teachings of the Buddha as understood within the Theravada tradition, the main focus of this book. I am deeply indebted to Geshe Lobsang Tharchin, my teacher within the Vajrayana tradition, although there is nothing of significance I could say in this short work about Vajrayana. I am very grateful to Professor Moreland Perkins for encouraging me to teach Buddhism as philosophy and for initiating the analytical investigations that frame the discussion of impermanence in Chapter 2 and provide the foundation for Chapter 8.

A number of people have helped to improve this book. Ajahn Pasanno, co-abbot of Abhayagiri, not only commented on the final draft but set aside time for several discussions of key points. Pali scholar Jakub Bartovsky commented on the Theravada chapters and used his translation skills to insure that all Pali translations were accurate and in good English. Bob and Val McKee, Dorly Mueller, and Chuck Yannaconne each made numerous comments that significantly improved the final version. The chapter on Vajrayana is substantially better thanks to Tibetan scholar Artemus Engle. To each of these persons the reader and I owe a debt of gratitude. What mistakes or misunderstandings persist are my own responsibility.

I thank Southern University Press for permission to use, as Chapter 8, a revision of my "The Possibility of Nonattachment," from *Buddhism And The Emerging World Civilization*, ed. Ramakrishna Puligandla and David L. Miller [(c) 1996 by the Board of Trustees, Southern Illinois University].

Finally, I am indebted to series editor Daniel Kolak for his invitation to write this book and for his encouragement along the way.

Abbreviations

A   *Anguttara-nikaya* [*The Book of Gradual Sayings*, trans. by F.L. Woodward]

D   *Digha-nikaya* [*Thus have I Heard*, trans. by Maurice Walshe; also an earlier translation by T.W. and C.A. F. Rhys Davids]

Dmp   *Dhammapada* [many translations available]

M   *Majjhima-nikaya* [*The Middle Length Discourses of the Buddha*, trans. By Bhikkhu Nanamoli and Bhikkhu Bodhi; also an earlier translation by I.B. Horner]

S   *Sanyutta-nikaya* [*The Book of Kindred Sayings*, trans. by C.A.F. Rhys Davids and F.L. Woodward]

Ud   *Udana* [*The Minor Anthologies of the Pali Canon*, Pt. II, trans. By F.L. Woodward]

Vin   *Vinaya Pitaka* [*The Book of the Discipline*, trans. by I.B. Honer]

Vsm   *Visuddhimagga*, by Bhadantacariya Buddhaghosa [*The Path of Purification*, trans. by Bhikkhu Nanamoli]

1

The Buddha

The name "Buddha" refers to a person who has awakened from the delusions of ordinary life and has discovered the nature of reality. The particular Buddha whose ideas we are to explore was born into the Sakya clan and was named Siddhattha Gotama. Gotama (Sanskrit is Gautama) came to see that life, for all its promise and hope, ended with dying and inevitably contained irritation, disappointment, and loss. Rather than being overwhelmed and depressed by the suffering in life, Gotama set out to discover a solution to it. This book is a reflective summary of his discovery.

The historical person whom we call the Buddha was a prince who was no more divine than any other human being. He was born in North India in the 6th century BC.[1] According to legend, an oracle told his parents that their child would be either a great king or a great spiritual leader. His father, wanting him to be a great king, asked what might cause his son to turn from being a great king into becoming a spiritual leader. The oracle told him that if his son saw the four signs that often cause people to be reflective about the human condition (old age, disease, death, and a wandering ascetic) he would retire from the worldly life. The king surrounded his son Gotama with luxury and gave orders that his son should not come in contact with any of the four signs. Despite his father's best attempts to keep his son distracted by luxury, Gotama conspired with his charioteer to explore beyond the palace walls and, in the course of these excursions, came upon a very elderly person, an extremely ill person, and a corpse. He came to realize that sickness, old age, and death were an inevitable part of human life. After he

1

saw wandering ascetics who had retired from the worldly life to seek liberation, he determined that he would do the same. Seeking to discover a solution to the problem of suffering, Gotama left the comforts of the princely life, leaving his wife and his son in the care of his parents.

Gotama began practicing meditation under meditation master Alara Kalama. Having reached the highest attainment that Alara Kalama himself had reached, Gotama left when he found that this attainment did not lead to peace, to direct realization, or to Nibbana (M: 26, 15). He next practiced with Uddaka Ramaputta and reached an even higher meditative state but left for the same reason (M: 26, 17). Going off on his own, he practiced the severest of yogic austerities for six years. During this period five ascetics joined him.

At the end of this six-year period Gotama almost died because of the severity of his practice. He came to the conclusion that an excessively emaciated body was not a means to enlightenment. He ate a meal of boiled rice and bread. When the five ascetics saw him eating rice and bread, they left in disgust thinking "Gotama now lives luxuriously; he has given up his striving and reverted to luxury" (M: 36, 33).

Gotama again went off on his own. He was thirty-five years old. He determined he would sit under a tree on the bank of the river Neranjara at the place now called Buddh Gaya until he had seen through delusion and solved the problem of suffering. During a night of intense and deep meditation he "woke up" and understood the nature of reality. The problem of suffering was solved. He was an awakened one, a "Buddha."

At first he believed he could not successfully convey his realization to others. The Buddha saw anything he taught would go against the worldly stream because most people live pursuing what is pleasurable and avoiding what they take to be unpleasant (M: 26, 19). Part of the problem, too, was that the Buddha's deepest insights were incapable in principle of being fully conveyed in words. Nonetheless, the Buddha realized that there were beings with "little dust in their eyes" whom he might try to teach. His first two choices were the meditation masters with whom he had practiced, Alara Kalama and Uddaka Ramaputta. Unfortunately, both had died. He chose, therefore, to try to convey what he could to the five ascetics who had left him when he ate the bread and boiled rice.

The Buddha walked to Benares, to the Deer Park at Isipatana, and approached the group of five. Although they were still uncertain about him because he had succumbed to the luxury of ordinary food, they greeted him warmly. He told them that he was enlightened. They did not believe it. After all, from their perspective he was living a life of luxury. Gotama told them he was not living luxuriously--was he not living the homeless life? They were still unbelieving, since his practice was not the strenuous asceticism to which they were accustomed. Finally he said to them, "Have you ever known me to speak like this before?" They agreed that they had not and so he began teaching them. What he taught that day in Deer Park at Benares has become the foundation of one of the oldest philosophical and religious traditions on earth.

The basic teachings of the Buddha point only to what can be experienced. The Buddha did not encourage beliefs in transcendental or metaphysical dogmas. He rejected all speculative reasoning and theorizing. He articulated no belief in a personal creator deity. The beginning and end of his teachings point to what each human being can experience. Throughout his life the Buddha emphasized direct realization by the individual. Even as he was dying, at the age of eighty years old, his last words to his disciples were that they should strive on tirelessly (D: 16, 6.7).

In this short work we investigate the central ideas of the Buddha. We will focus on the teachings of the Buddha taught today as Theravada Buddhism.[2] There are other schools of Buddhism that we will discuss in the final three chapters: Mahayana Buddhism, Zen Buddhism, and Vajrayana. Since each of these forms of Buddhism is rooted in the basic historical teachings of the Buddha, our focus on Theravada Buddhism will be useful even for the reader whose primary interest is in one of these other forms of Buddhism.

In the next chapter we will begin with the Buddha's first teaching and the effect it had on one of those who, upon hearing it, saw deeply into the nature of all phenomena.

----

1. The Buddha lived about eighty years. The best estimates of the dates for his life vary. According to several western scholars, the Buddha lived from 563 to 483B.C., whereas Sri Lankans and others in SE Asia maintain that 623(or 624) to 543(or 544)B.C. are the proper dates. Whatever are the exact dates, the teachings of the Buddha have been taught and practiced continually for over two thousand five hundred years.

2. 'Theravada' means 'the teaching of the Elders' [vada (teaching) of the Elders (thera)].

3

2

The First Teaching

The Buddha sought out his former companions to attempt to convey what he had realized, for they were not caught up in worldly pursuits and might understand. The Buddha taught four insights that are true for each of us, rich or poor, university professor or death row prisoner, young or old. These four statements stand out to such an extent against the backdrop of our individual dramas that the Buddha called them the Four Noble Truths.

In the Four Noble Truths the Buddha shares his discovery of the solution to the problem of suffering. When the Buddha refers to suffering (the Pali word is 'dukkha'), he refers not only to overwhelming suffering, but also to unease, disappointment, stress, irritation, and feelings of unsatisfactoriness:

> Now this, monks, is the noble truth of suffering: Birth is suffering, aging is suffering, death is suffering; sorrow, lamentation, pain, dejection, and despair are suffering; association with the disliked is suffering, separation from the loved is suffering, not to obtain what we desire is suffering. In short, the five aggregates affected by clinging are suffering.

> And this, monks, is the noble truth of the origination of suffering: the craving which causes the renewal of becoming, is accompanied by sensual delight and seeks satisfaction now here, now there: that is to say, the craving for sensual pleasure, the craving for becoming, the craving for non-becoming.

4

And this, monks, is the noble truth of the cessation of suffering: the remainderless fading and cessation, renunciation, relinquishment, release, and letting go of craving.

And this, monks, is the noble truth of the way of practice leading to the cessation of suffering, the Noble Eightfold Path: right understanding, right attitude, right speech, right action, right livelihood, right effort, right mindfulness, and right concentration (S: LVI, XII, ii).

After the first sermon, one of his former companions, the Elder Kondanna, realized that whatsoever is an arising thing, all that is a ceasing thing.[1]

Impermanence

When the Elder Kondanna realized the impermanence of all "arising" phenomena (hereafter, all conditioned phenomena), the Buddha knew that Kondanna had understood. Since the insight into the impermanence of all conditioned phenomena is a fundamental insight of the Buddha's teaching, we will ask whether the statement expressing this insight is true and, to the degree to which it is true, what it tells us about our lives.

Before we try to determine whether this statement is true, we need to clarify its meaning. The statement is: whatsoever is an arising thing, all that is a ceasing thing. One meaning of this statement is that whatever has a beginning has an end. Notice that this statement does not mean or imply that everything must end, but only that those things that have beginnings will end. A second meaning of this statement is that, to the degree to which something has come into existence, to that degree it is already in the process of ending. In examining whether the statement expressing impermanence is true, we will use the first meaning: does everything that begins, end?

Although everything we see, touch, taste, smell and feel ends, there is more in the universe than what we experience through our senses. Philosophical inquiry extends beyond the obvious. Since a primary method of philosophically examining whether a statement is true is to try to discover something that shows it false, we will try to find a counterexample to the statement that whatsoever is an arising thing, all that is a ceasing thing.

It may seem, initially, that because the first law of thermodynamics tells us that the energy of the universe will never end, the energy of the universe is a successful counterexample. But the same law of thermodynamics states that the energy of the universe was never created. It follows that the energy of the universe fails to be a counterexample because the statement that what begins, ends, only refers to what had a beginning.

Other potential counterexamples are more intriguing. Consider the law of gravity. It was first articulated by Isaac Newton and it will always be true, so it may seem to be something that has a beginning and does not have an ending. But does the law of gravity have a beginning? Either Newton invented the law of gravity or he discovered it. Insofar as Newton invented this law and gave it a beginning, this law is an idea that will exist only as long as people are able to think it. Millions of years before the earth is consumed by an ever-expanding sun, there will be no people to think this idea and, as an idea that Newton invented, it will cease. We typically believe, however, that Newton did not invent the law of gravity, but that he discovered it. Insofar as Newton discovered this law, this law describes a characteristic of energy and, like energy itself, neither begins nor ends.

There is a potential counterexample that has more staying power. If there are individual immortal souls, as many people believe, then we have found a counterexample to the statement that whatever begins, ends, for immortal souls have a beginning and never cease. How are we to determine whether this counterexample defeats the statement that whatever begins, ends? Should we try to resolve whether there are individual immortal souls?

Trying to resolve the question of immortal souls would immediately land us in an endless morass of argumentation, theorizing, refutation, and speculation. We could devote the rest of this short book, and many more, to pursuing the complexities of this question and would not satisfactorily resolve the issue. After reading whatever was written, some would believe there are immortal souls, others would believe there are none, and some would be unsure How, then, should we proceed to assess this potential counterexample to the statement that whatever begins, ends?

Metaphysical Questions

The question of whether there are individual immortal souls is a metaphysical question. It is a question that we cannot resolve by empirical investigation, plausibly not even by any examination or investigation of our experience. As we can already tell, this question is a potential showstopper that can derail an exploration of what insight the Buddha may have had into solving the problem of suffering. Yet the reason the question is a potential showstopper is exactly the reason we need to set it aside. The Buddha's response to questions raised by Malunkyaputta, one of his followers, makes this point clearly.

Malunkyaputta asked the Buddha ten metaphysical questions, threatening to stop following the Buddha if he refused to answer them.[2] In his response, the Buddha begins by reminding Malunkyaputta that he never promised to answer any metaphysical questions and that all he teaches is suffering, its origin, its cessation, and the way out of suffering. He then tells a story in which he compares Malunkyaputta to a man wounded by a poisoned arrow. The victim's friends, relatives and neighbors bring a surgeon to treat the man. The victim says,

> I will not let the surgeon pull out this arrow until I know the name and clan of the man who wounded me; . . . whether the man who wounded me was tall or short or of middle height . . . was dark or brown or golden-skinned . . . lives in such a village or town or city; . . . whether the bow . . . was a long bow or a crossbow; . . . whether the bowstring . . . was fibre or reed or sinew or hemp or bark; . . . whether the shaft that wounded me was wild or cultivated; . . . with what kind of feathers the shaft that wounded me was fitted--whether those of a vulture or a crow or a hawk or a peacock or a stork; . . . with what kind of sinew the shaft that wounded me was bound--whether that of an ox or a buffalo or a lion or a monkey; . . . until I know what kind of arrow it was that wounded me--whether it was hoof-tipped or curved or barbed or calf-toothed . . . (M: 63, 5).

The Buddha tells Malunkyaputta that the victim would die before he friends, family and neighbors could answer all his questions. Likewise, anyone who waited for the Buddha to answer metaphysical questions would die because the Buddha does not make metaphysical statements. Instead, the Buddha concludes his talk with Malunkyaputta by pointing out what he teaches:

> What have I declared? "This is suffering"--I have declared. "This is the origin of suffering"--I have declared. "This is the cessation of suffering"--I have declared. "This is the way leading to the cessation of suffering"--I have declared. Why have I declared that? Because it is beneficial, it belongs to the fundamentals of the holy life, it leads to disenchantment, to dispassion, to cessation, to peace, to direct knowledge, to enlightenment, to Nibbana. That is why I have declared it (M: 63, 9-10).

7

This is not the way we expect a spiritual founder to answer metaphysical questions. We are accustomed to statements, pronouncements, theories, justification, and requirements about what we should believe. The Buddha set all this aside as having nothing to do with the holy life.

The Buddha, during his forty-five years of teaching, never answered any of the ten metaphysical questions. In his conversation with Malunkyaputta, the Buddha explained with a simile. On another occasion he warned that holding metaphysical views is "a thicket of views" causing vexation "and does not lead to... peace, to direct knowledge, to enlightenment, to Nibbana" (M: 72.14). On yet another question, confronted with metaphysical questions, the Buddha simply remained silent (S: XLIV, X, 10). In all these ways the Buddha eschewed metaphysical views and the discussion of metaphysical views. In place of views, the Buddha taught the importance of the "actual vision" of the nature, origin and cessation of all conditioned phenomena (M: 72.15). The Buddha taught that it is only by letting go of all supposings, all imaginings, and all tendencies to claiming views as "mine" that a person can be delivered and see truth directly.

Like Malunkyaputta, we probably prefer to have all our questions answered, however metaphysical. But, as the Buddha pointed out, resolving metaphysical questions at the level of discourse is an endless pursuit. We can learn from the Buddha's advice to Malunkyaputta as we return to the question of whether the existence of immortal souls is a counterexample to the statement that whatsoever is an arising thing, all that is a ceasing thing. Obviously we are not going to reach any consensus or other resolution of the metaphysical question about immortal souls. How, then, should we proceed to examine the statement to which it is a possible counterexample?

The answer is that we can change our question without trying to resolve what we cannot resolve at the level of discussion. Instead of asking whether it is true that whatever begins, ends, we will ask: to what degree is this statement true?

Impermanence Revisited

Although we can not determine the truth of the statement that whatever begins, ends, as far as controversial metaphysical views are concerned, at the level of our everyday lives we know a great deal about the truth of this statement. In particular, we know with certainty that it is true of everything in our everyday experience. Our health, the well-being of those we love, relationships, jobs, school, youth, all of this began and we know all of it will cease. When we examine our activities, our hopes, how we dress, what we say, what we do, most of us will find that most if not all of our activities, our thinking, and our concerns have nothing to do with anything that is not impermanent. Yet, as a text reminds us, "all that is mine, all that is beloved and pleasing, will someday be otherwise, will someday be separated from me"(AN: iii, 71-72). Beyond any reasonable doubt, Kondanna's insight into impermanence applies in a profound way to our daily lives.

What follows from the degree to which conditioned phenomena are impermanent? Does it follow that human life is depressing? Or does the truth make us free? A short reflection at this juncture may be useful. If a truth is depressing, likely we had hopes, expectations, or attachments that this truth has undermined. For example, a gardener is not depressed when the golden sage she planted continues growing in the spring, but if it died during the winter and she was expecting it to be alive the following spring, she might be depressed. Similarly, the impermanence of conditioned phenomena depresses us only if we expected our bodies, our loved ones, and our possessions to last forever. Someone who lacked these expectations would be unlikely to be depressed by the Buddha's observations.

Our illusory expectations can, and do, cause us to feel depressed when they conflict with reality. When we do not have illusory expectations, endings do not depress us. For example, we are not depressed that a sunset ends, that a kiss ends, that a meal ends, that a movie ends, or that a meditation period ends--in fact we would likely be quite distressed if any of these failed to end. If we have a deep insight into impermanence, it is possible that we might come to be able to abide the ending of anything with the equanimity that we now abide the ending of a sunset or a meal. Whether that possibility is plausible will be a question that we will answer as we explore in detail the teachings of the Buddha.

----

1. Although this realization is sometimes translated as I do above, it is more literally translated: whatever is subject (liable) to arising, all that is subject (liable) to cessation. I use the less literal translation in the text because, after analysis, it refers to the same feature of conditioned phenomena while allowing for a clearer discussion.

2. The ten questions are whether: (I) the world is eternal, (ii) the world is not eternal, (iii) the world is finite, (iv) the world is infinite, (v) the soul is the same as the body, (vi) the soul is one thing and the body another, (vii) after death a Tathagata exists, (viii) after death a Tathagata does not exist, (ix) after death a Tathagata both exists and does not exist, and (ix) after death a Tathagata neither exists nor does not exist. (M: 63, 3)

3

The Way Out of Suffering

The Four Noble Truths, the heart of the Buddha's teaching, provide a framework for a lifetime of reflection.[1] Throughout his forty-five years of teaching the Buddha taught these Noble Truths to guide others along the path out of suffering. In this chapter we briefly examine each of them.

Understanding Suffering

The Buddha began with the fact of suffering, an experience he knew was familiar to his five former companions. The Buddha spoke not only to them when he stated the First Noble Truth, but to each of us:

> Birth is suffering, aging is suffering, death is suffering; sorrow, lamentation, pain, dejection, and despair are suffering; association with the disliked is suffering, separation from the loved is suffering, not to obtain what we desire is suffering. In short, the five aggregates affected by clinging are suffering.

The Buddha adds that this First Noble Truth had three aspects: that this is the truth of suffering, that suffering is to be understood, and that suffering has been understood. To appreciate the philosophy of the Buddha, we need to examine what it means to understand suffering.

To understand suffering does not require becoming an expert on neurological reactions, or on pain control, or on theories about suffering. Rather, it means to come to understand suffering within one's own experience. Yet on the face of it we seem to understand suffering only too well. We know it hurts. We do not like it. What more do we need to know? That is why we use painkillers, antidepressants, or drugs like alcohol. We understand it and we want it gone.

Although we may think we understand suffering, it is difficult to understand something towards which we have such aversion. Once suffering is present, we are not inclined to investigate it. We want to be rid of it and often we do whatever is necessary to get rid of it. We take the suffering to be "mine" and we want it gone. In fact, when we experience especially powerful forms of suffering--e.g., someone we love dying or being told we have a life-threatening illness--we may even wonder what we did wrong, or whether we are somehow responsible. Because suffering and death affect innocent children, some argue that there cannot be a God who is omnipotent and good, or else such things would not happen. In short, we take a very personal perspective toward suffering and want to blame someone.

The Buddha's statement of the First Noble Truth does not take a personal perspective. The Buddha did not say "we suffer" or "each of us suffers" and then point to birth, illness, separation, death, and all the rest. Instead, he said "there is suffering." He did not say it was mine or yours or that it belonged to anyone. He did not blame suffering on anyone. The First Noble Truth makes a straightforward observation: there is suffering. In the same natural way that rain occurs, winds blow, and the sun rises and sets daily, so too suffering occurs as a part of the web of life.

When we take this perspective--letting go of responsibility, blame, aversion and no longer thinking of suffering as "mine" or "me"-- it is easier to begin to understand suffering. The English word 'understand' happens to provide a useful hint here: to "stand" "under." To understand suffering we need to experience it directly. Metaphorically speaking, we need to stand under it in order to investigate it. We are more able to understand suffering when we take the perspective that it is just one of the many phenomena in the range of our experience. From this perspective we are more able to investigate a physical pain or any negative psychological phenomenon. Consider a feeling of disappointment. We can investigate whether it has a physical location, how it changes, whether it is associated with pressure or sharpness or warmth or any other physical aspect. We can also explore physical pains and negative moods, like depression, using the same investigative perspective to explore their varied aspects. In short, as we abandon the personal perspective for an investigative perspective, we are more able to investigate dukkha and so come to understand it.

The First Noble Truth ends with the clause "the five aggregates affected by clinging are suffering." These five categories, which we explore in the next chapter, are the categories the Buddha used to analyze what we are as persons. By referring to these five categories the Buddha is pointing out that suffering is a feature of the human condition. It is as natural as breathing and eating. There is nothing personal about it. Why does an innocent child suffer? Because the child was born and suffering is part of the human condition. Suffering follows upon birth.[2]

Abandoning Desire

The suffering referred to in the First Noble Truth covers a whole range of suffering: severe physical suffering, intense psychological suffering, as well as minor irritations and annoyances. The word 'dukkha' in the Pali texts that is often translated as 'suffering'[3] includes disappointment, sadness, tension, depression, uneasiness, feeling hurt, as well as grief, fear, terror, and anguish. According to the Buddha, dukkha has craving as its cause:

> And this, monks, is the noble truth of the origination of suffering: the craving which causes the renewal of becoming, is accompanied by sensual delight and seeks satisfaction now here, now there: that is to say, the craving for sensual pleasure, the craving for becoming, the craving for non-becoming.

The Buddha adds that this noble truth has three aspects: that suffering has an origin, that desire should be abandoned, and that desire has been abandoned. In our discussion of this Second Noble Truth, we will use the word 'desire' for 'craving' since each accurately translates the Pali.[4]

The emphasis on desire may seem puzzling, for it seems to contradict the First Noble Truth which cites a host of factors that we know are able to cause suffering: birth, aging, illness, death, and so on. We plausibly would not suffer if the conditions mentioned in the First Noble Truth never occurred. Obviously we would not suffer if we were not born but, assuming birth, we would not seem vulnerable to suffering if no one aged or became sick, if we were never dissociated from the loved, if we always got what we wanted, if we never had to experience what we did not like, and if we never experienced dejection, despair, sorrow, or grief. Why would the Buddha point to desire as the cause of suffering when everything else is what seems to go awry?

We cannot prevent death, we cannot stop aging, we cannot effectively prevent all illnesses. These factors of the human condition are unavoidable. Even suicide, which may seem a way to avoid some of these conditions, only hastens others. We cannot eliminate or control all the factors and processes that cause suffering. Even if we could control the gross material world and prevent death and aging and even sickness, we would face conflicts of desires among individuals that could not be resolved. Suppose, for example, that Ron wants to spend the evening alone with Judy, but Judy wants to spend the evening with someone else. There is simply no arrangement of material phenomena that could satisfy these conflicting desires.

This puzzlement over the Second Noble Truth rests on the fact that there are many causal factors contributing to the arising of suffering. What the Buddha implicitly points out in the Second Noble Truth is that we can effectively do something about only one of these factors. Against a background of conditions which cannot be avoided, desire, the one factor about which we can do something, is properly identified as the cause of suffering. Because desire is always a causal factor when suffering occurs, and because the Buddha's purpose is to solve the problem of suffering, it is appropriate to identify, as the cause of suffering, the one factor about which we can do something.

An example clarifies the logic of identifying only one of several causal factors as the cause of dukkha. Consider the question: what causes the fire in the barn when the fire follows upon someone lighting a match? We say that lighting the match caused the fire, but other causal factors are also required: oxygen, fuel, and a lack of moisture. Since these three conditions are typical in barns and so are part of the background conditions, we look to the factor over which we have control given these background conditions and we identify that factor as the cause of the fire. If we want to solve the problem of barnfires under normal conditions, then we identify lighting matches as the cause of fire rather than any of the background conditions of oxygen, fuel, and a lack of moisture. Likewise, the factors of birth, sickness, separation, and death that are inherent in human life are the background against which we look for a causal factor which contributes to suffering and about which we can do something. That factor is desire, and against the inevitable conditions of human existence, we identify it as the cause of suffering.

The Buddha refers to three kinds of desire: the desire to get (craving for sensual pleasure), the desire to become (craving for becoming), and the desire to avoid (craving for non-becoming). From the perspective of someone trying to solve the problem of suffering, these are its cause.

When we desire to get something, it will be either something that we perceive as transient--for instance, a meal or a concert--or something that we take to be permanent. With those objects that we perceive as transient, either we satisfy our desire or we fail to satisfy our desire. If we fail to satisfy our desire, there will typically be suffering, from mild disappointment to anguish, depending on the degree of intensity of the unsatisfied desire. On the other hand, if we satisfy our desire for what is transient, there typically is a period of pleasure, relaxation, or contentment. But, importantly, our expectations are generally raised for "more and better" on the next occasion. For example, the instant coffee that satisfied us when we first drank coffee would likely taste awful to us now, the first romantic kiss we experienced would likely no longer have the same impact, and our tastes are probably too refined to be satisfied with anything except the sound produced by a CD or a vinyl record in mint condition. As our tastes become more refined, our desires become more difficult to satisfy. The result is an ever-increasing likelihood of disappointment.

When we turn to desires for what we perceive to be permanent, the logic of the reflection moves quickly. When we think about our own health, the well-being of those we love, jobs, reputations, or anything that we take to be permanent, the impermanence of all conditioned phenomena shows that we will eventually lose everything that we take to be ours, if only when we die. This is the way it is and the way it has been for everybody before us.

The desire to avoid is much like the desire to get, except that we want to get rid of something. We work hard at getting rid of what we do not want. We consume pharmaceuticals to get rid of pain, take tranquilizers to smooth out our feelings, drink alcohol to blur our grief, and watch television or videos to distract ourselves from anxiety or boredom. We use skin creams, deodorants, perfumes, hair implants, and even hire plastic surgeons to get rid of bodily features that do not fit an image. We also work hard at getting rid of external conditions that we find aversive, troublesome, competitive, or plain annoying. Some of us aim to be in positions of authority over others, many try to be managers or professionals less answerable to authority, others become hermits, still others develop refined skills of manipulation that can include charm, gossip, bribery, slander, threats, lying, and even violence. The aim, always, is to control, to get rid of, to avoid dukkha.

The desire to become is more subtle, in part because it is so pervasive. We desire to become students, professionals, monks, farmers, friends, lovers, as well as desire to be good or even best at whatever we are aiming to

14

become. When we are concerned with self-image, we are enmeshed in the desire to become. Yet whenever we become something, usually we desire to be better at it, or want to become something different, or want to remain the same in the future. Each of these becomings tends to lead to an attachment and an identification to what we have become. The desire to become in all these ways breeds further desires that make us even more vulnerable to frustration, will eventually be frustrated, if only at death, and takes our attention away from what is happening in the moment.

Although the Second Noble Truth states that desire is the cause of suffering, the aim is to abandon desire, not to annihilate it. The Buddha pointed to this aim in the second aspect of this Noble Truth: desire is to be abandoned. Abandoning desire is not annihilating it. The Buddha did not say that desire needed to be annihilated and that desire had been annihilated.[5] He said that desire should be abandoned and that desire had been abandoned.

Abandoning desire is not attaching to it, is letting go of it, is simply letting it be as if it were just another energy flowing through the body. The following first-person report provides an introductory illustration:

> I had walked out of the meditation hall after the ten-day retreat and went over to a display of audio tapes on meditation when an attractive woman came and stood next to me. I felt the energy of mutual attraction. My initial inclination was to ask her to go for a walk. Before I could put my inclination into action, I remembered I had gotten engaged shortly before the retreat. An immediate impulse arose--to push away the energy of attraction. At that instant it dawned on me--this was exactly the kind of situation for which I had been in training during the retreat. I tried out what I'd learned. I didn't act on the desire, I didn't repress it, but I simply watched the energies of attraction flow through my system. Had I acted on those energies, I wouldn't have watched them. Had I repressed them, I couldn't have watched them. Instead, by not acting on them and by not repressing them, I was able to watch them as they moved through my body and eventually ceased.[6]

Abandoning desire is just letting it go. It is not getting rid of, not suppression, and not denial. It is, instead, just letting be. We all know what desire does when we let it be: it ceases, as do all phenomena. When we suppress desire, or when we act it out, we instead reinforce the underlying habits of mind as well as lose the opportunity to investigate them.

The Middle Way between acting out and repression is not a path well understood in the West. Yet, as the Buddha points out in the second and third aspect to the Second Noble Truth, this is an integral part of the path out of suffering. To integrate the Second Noble Truth into one's life a person needs to let go of desire, to abandon it, to let it be. To do that requires not taking desire personally but as a phenomenon to be investigated.

What would it be like to let go of the three types of desires to get, to avoid, and to become? We would be fully attentive in the moment, without any attachment to its being improved or to ourselves being different. This does not mean that we would not act,[7] but it does mean that, whatever we did, we would do it without attachment. Without attachment to desire, suffering would cease: that is the Third Noble Truth.

The Cessation of Suffering

The Third Noble Truth points to Nibbana:

> And this, monks, is the noble truth of the cessation of suffering: the remainderless fading and cessation, renunciation, relinquishment, release, and letting go of craving.

Like each of the first two Noble Truths, the third has three aspects: that suffering has a cessation, that the cessation of suffering is to be realized, and that the cessation of suffering has been realized.

To realize the third Noble Truth requires that we need to be fully mindful of cessation. As difficult as it is to be attentive to suffering, as difficult as it is to let go of desire, these difficulties pale in comparison with the difficulty of being fully attentive to cessations. Cessations are not exciting and do not demand our attention. One moment we are filled with desire or suffering, the next we are thinking about something else. We pay little or no attention to cessations and, yet, to fulfill all three aspects of the Third Noble Truth, we must realize the cessation of suffering.

The Third Noble Truth, by pointing to cessation, points to Nibbana. The word 'nibbana' literally means 'to become extinguished'. The realization of nibbana refers to an insight or realization that cannot adequately be expressed in words. To try to talk about Nibbana is to attempt to cross the limits of language. The phenomena we can describe in language, whether material or psychological, are all part of the conditioned realm.

On those few occasions when the Buddha did say more about the goal of the practice, he called it the unconditioned. The Buddha's statements about the unconditioned are the nearest we get to a transcendental statement in Theravada Buddhism, and they are in terms of what the unconditioned is not:

> Monks, there is a not-born, a not-become, a not-made, a not-compounded. Monks, if that unborn, not-become, not-made, not-compounded were not, there would be apparent no escape from this here that is born, become, made, compounded. But since, monks, there is an unborn, not-become, not-made, not-compounded, therefore the escape from this here that is born, become, made, compounded is apparent. (Ud: 80-81.)

We tend to project superlative features onto what the realization of Nibbana must be like but, in fact, there is nothing that anyone can say about it, at least in positive terms that would convey any accurate meaning. We can say what it is not: it is not born, it is not suffering, it is not conditioned.[8] We cannot, however, say what it is. Positively the insight into Nibbana is ineffable: incapable in principle of being successfully conveyed in words.

It is worth noting that the Third Noble Truth answers the complaint that the Buddha's teachings are pessimistic. Although there is suffering, suffering has a cessation. That is not a pessimistic assessment. Instead, it is quite optimistic and hopeful, especially when compared with many philosophical and religious views that describe human life as a vale of tears and point to the possibility of happiness only in another realm. The Buddha, in contrast, lays out a path that leads in this life to the cessation of suffering, to Nibbana, to the unconditioned (M: 140, 25-31).

The Way Out of Suffering

As we saw in the First Noble Truth, the Buddha bluntly delineated the scope of the problem: every aspect of human life is enmeshed in a web that inevitably involves suffering. Although suffering is the problem, it is also the symptom of an underlying malady that causes the suffering. The diagnosis of this malady is given in the Second Noble Truth: desire is the cause of this symptom. The Third Noble Truth gives the prognosis: suffering can and does cease. The Fourth Noble Truth provides the therapeutic program that resolves the problem of suffering:

And this, monks, is the noble truth of the way of practice leading to the cessation of suffering, the Noble Eightfold Path: right understanding, right attitude, right speech, right action, right livelihood, right effort, right mindfulness, and right concentration.

The Fourth Noble Truth, like the first three, has three aspects: that there is this path, that this path must be cultivated, and that this path has been cultivated. The aim of this path is to realize the ultimate nature of reality. The path is traditionally divided into three sections:

> The Wisdom Components of the Path:
> 1. Right Understanding
> 2. Right Attitude
> The Moral Components of the Path:
> 3. Right Speech
> 4. Right Action
> 5. Right Livelihood
> The Concentration Components of the Path:
> 6. Right Effort
> 7. Right Mindfulness
> 8. Right Concentration.

Although the Buddha expressed the Eightfold Path as a list, it does not follow that one first develops Right Understanding, then Right Attitude, and so forth seriatim down the list. The list is only a method of presentation. Each factor needs to be developed. In practice one will sometimes emphasize a particular factor or find oneself in a situation in which a particular factor applies, but the essential point is that all need to be developed. Consider a list of what is needed for growing a plant: seed, soil, water, nutrients, sunlight, and temperature. In providing a list of what is necessary for a plant to grow, we have no choice but to state one item and then another. Yet each of these factors must be present and in the right amount or the plant will fail to flourish.

The Buddha did not claim to have invented the Eightfold path. Instead, he claimed only to have rediscovered it:

> Just as if, monks, a man faring through the forest through the great wood should see an ancient path, an ancient road traversed by men of former days . . . Even so have I seen an ancient path, an ancient road traversed by the fully enlightened ones of former times. And

what, monks, is that ancient path?... right understanding, right attitude, right speech, right action, right livelihood, right effort, right mindfulness, right concentration. This is that ancient path, that ancient road, traversed by the fully enlightened ones of former times (S: XII, 7, 65).

Although the Buddha claimed he did not invent this path, he does seem to be the first person who described it, for we find no mention of the Eightfold Path in any prior documents or teachings.

No Dogmas To Believe

Neither the Four Noble Truths nor the Eightfold Path are dogmas or views that need to believed. Rather, these are reflections and guidelines that need to be tested. The Buddha encouraged exactly this investigative approach during his visit with the Kalamas.

The Kalamas told the Buddha about their predicament--that many teachers visited them, each propounding his own views and berating the views of the others. The Buddha responded by praising their doubt, telling them that their "doubt has arisen precisely about what ought to be doubted." He told them not to be satisfied with hearsay or tradition but to rely on their own knowledge. "When you know in yourselves that certain things are unwholesome," he told them, "you should give them up." On the other hand, when they know some things to be wholesome, they should "accept them and follow them"(AN: III, 65). On another occasion, the Buddha told an inquirer that he should use whatever he sees or hears to investigate the Buddha himself (M: 47, 4).

This investigative stance is the perspective of someone who is searching for the truth about reality and about how to live. When we take this perspective we do not grasp and become attached even to the Four Noble Truths or the Eightfold Path. Like all phenomena, they are but conditions and, however important and useful they may be, they are only tools that we may be able to use to realize the ultimate nature of reality and to liberate ourselves from suffering.

The Buddha tells his followers that his teachings are "similar to a raft, for the purpose of crossing over, not for the purpose of grasping"(M: 38, 14). There is no wisdom in attaching to the vehicle used for making the crossing. "Suppose," the Buddha says, "a man in the course of a journey saw a great expanse of water, whose near shore was dangerous and fearful and whose further shore was safe and free from fear, but there was no ferryboat or bridge going to the far shore." The Buddha asks us to imagine that this man collects branches and twigs and leaves and binds them together into a raft with which he crosses to the other shore. After this person successfully crosses to the other side, what should he do with the raft? Because it was so useful to him, should he carry it with him wherever he goes? No, says the Buddha, what he should do is abandon the raft and set forth on his journey. "I have shown you how the Dhamma is similar to a raft, being for the purpose of crossing over, not for the purpose of grasping" (M: 22, 13).

----

1. Ajahn Sumedho, *The Four Noble Truths* (Great Gaddesden, England: Amaravati Publications, 1992), p. 13.

2. Ajahn Sumedho, *Now Is The Knowing* (Great Gaddesden, England: Amaravati Publications, 1996), p. 34.

3. The translations from the late nineteenth century and the beginning of the twentieth century translated the word 'dukkha' not only as 'suffering', but also as 'ill'. Contemporary translations of 'dukkha' include, in addition to 'suffering', 'dis-ease', 'stress', and 'unsatisfactoriness'.

4. I use 'craving' in translations of the texts, since that translation is more customary and widespread. For an example of 'tanha' translated as 'desire', see Sucitto Bhikkhu, *The Dawn of the Dhamma* (Bangkok: Buddhadhamma Foundation, 1996), pp. xxvii, 32, and passim.

5. There are translations in which the language of annihilation and destruction is used but, as far as I can tell, these translations are erroneous. For a recent discussion on what is meant by the "cessation" (nirodha) or desire, see the end of Chapter 4 below. Implicit in understanding the cesssation of desire is the following question: whether a desire, to which there is neither attachment nor aversion, and which, furthermore, produces no disposition or tendency to act, is still a desire, or only a feeling.

6. The author of this report has requested anonymity and permitted me to edit it for this book.

7. This will be discussed thoroughly below in Chapter 8.

8. This is analogous to the well-known "via negativa" of Western mysticism which is a method used to point to what is ineffable by negating all relevant terms that refer to entities or features in the conditioned realm.

4

Self and Not-Self

The question of what or who we are is a profound philosophical question that permeates ordinary thinking. For example, when someone befriends a person, that person may wonder whether the new friend really likes her or, instead, likes her money, her looks, or her connections. These familiar questions show that we do distinguish between an idea of a more real self and aspects of ourselves that others mistakenly may take to be who we are.

The Buddha's approach to the nature of the self extends this natural familiar mode of thinking. The Buddha knew that we are not our money, not our job, and not our social connections. He knew this for the same reason we do: we can be aware of our money, we can be aware of our job, we can be aware of our social connections and that awareness is separate from each and all of these conditions. If we can be aware of some phenomenon, then we can distinguish between the phenomenon and the awareness of it. We intuitively take the awareness to be more truly ourselves than those conditions that are the objects of awareness. The conclusion from this benign reflection is radical. Since there can be awareness of every phenomenon that we might use to identify ourselves, it follows that none of those phenomena is who or what we really are.

In the First Noble Truth the Buddha cites the five basic factors with which human beings tend to identify: body, feeling, perceptions, mental formations, and sense consciousness. These five components of human beings are called "the five aggregates" and constitute what we take ourselves and others to be on the conventional level.

21

The Five Aggregates

The first aggregate, body, includes what we ordinarily mean by 'body'--limbs, head, body parts--as well as all the material energies that compose a body in all its various functions and manifestations: heat, movement, pressure, and tingling. The second aggregate, feeling, includes feelings of pleasantness, unpleasantness, and neutrality. Perception, the third aggregate, includes memory and refers to the mental function of making sense out of raw, unnamed experiences. It is the "recognizing" function of the mind: we identify a visual impression as a shape (one perception), as a long brown shape (a more refined perception), as a snake (yet further refined), and then as a rope (yet another perception). This "recognizing" function also works when we identify inner phenomena. For example, I may feel a pressure in my solar plexus, take it to be indigestion, and later come to perceive it as a physical correlate of fear. The fourth aggregate of mental formations includes volitional activities: willing, thinking, imagining, and other mental and intentional activities. Scholars translate the Pali word for the fifth aggregate with the word 'consciousness', although in English this is misleading since the words 'consciousness' and 'awareness' have overlapping meanings. The fifth aggregate refers to the various ways in which we take in raw, unidentified experiences or sensations: eye consciousness, ear consciousness, nose consciousness, tongue consciousness, body consciousness, and mind consciousness.

What is remarkable about these five aggregates is that they do not just form a list in an ancient philosophical system that students need to memorize but has no relevance to our lives or what we are as human beings. Instead, the five aggregates constitute all the experiential aspects of what we are. Everything about us as persons is found among the five aggregates.[1]

Beyond the Five Aggregates

Our deepest questions about the nature and the identity of who and what we are will plausibly not be answered by the claim that the five aggregates constitute the person. If I am nothing more than the five aggregates, then what or who is aware of them? If I am nothing but these five aggregates and each of these is in the process of change, then what makes me the same person year after year? We begin discussing these questions by exploring what makes each of us the same person year after year.

When we identify ourselves or others on the everyday level of social relations and personal histories, we use conventional criteria to determine who we are. For example, if I am able to remember an event from five years ago, I assume I am the same person as the person who experienced the event. Or when Annette is able to remember details that could only be known by a person named Annette who witnessed an event ten years ago, we assume that today's Annette is identical with the Annette who witnessed the event. In each of these examples we are applying the criterion of memory to establish personal identity. We also use the criterion of bodily identity to establish personal identity. For example, when Kathy shows her passport to the authorities, they can tell from looking at Kathy that she fits the physical description in the passport and that she looks like a later version of the person in the passport photograph. Having established, within reasonable parameters, the bodily identity of the person before them and the person named in the passport, they conclude that the person before them is Kathy.

On the conventional level of everyday life, we use both the criteria of body and memory to identify persons. Yet these conventional identities, based on memory and bodily continuity, establish the existence of a person over time only on a conventional level. Annette may be identified as the Annette who existed ten years earlier, but is there an Annette who has existed continuously for those ten years? The answer is that Annette both did and did not exist for those ten years.

Although this may seem like doubletalk, this is the way it is with houses, forests, fires, and persons. Many, even all of the parts of an entity might change and yet the entity might be numerically the same as a predecessor. Consider an old man and the child who he had been, the ancient redwood and the seedling from which it grew, a wooden boat that has had every piece replaced during its hundred-year existence, or a prairie fire that is numerically one fire even though nothing, including its location, may remain exactly the same. That is how it is with all conditioned entities. Although nothing is exactly the same, former manifestations are numerically identical with later manifestations. Numerical identity is consistent with some constituents of a thing changing, most constituents changing, and sometimes even all of the constituents of a thing changing--think of the prairie fire or the boat that is rebuilt time and time again until no original piece is left. The identity of a person over time is only numerical identity and so allows for change.

The inability to discover some underlying personal continuant was clearly stated by Scottish philosopher David Hume. Hume was a keen observer and saw, like the Buddha, that there was nothing in the realm of phenomena that could be considered a self and that continued over time. Reflecting on the ideas and impressions that arise in our minds, which Hume called perceptions, Hume wrote:

> The mind is a kind of theatre, where several perceptions successively make their appearance; pass, re-pass, glide away, and mingle in an infinite variety of postures and situations. There is properly no *simplicity* in it at any one time, nor identity in *different*; whatever natural propension we may have to imagine that simplicity and identity. The comparison of the theatre must not mislead us. They are the successive perceptions only, that constitute the mind; nor have we the most distant notion of the place, where these scenes are presented, or of the materials, of which it is compos'd.[2]

Hume's observation involves our direct awareness of, and ideas about, each of the five aggregates. Look as hard as one may, there is nothing to be found that is not changing and so none that could be a continuing self.

More than two thousand years before Hume, in his second major teaching to the five ascetics, the Buddha taught that each of the five aggregates is "anatta," or not-self (Vin: I, 13-14). Anatta is one of the central teachings of the Buddha, and the Buddha often emphasized the importance of anatta as a tool leading to ultimate liberation. The following is from a conversation between the Buddha and his son Rahula, who by this time had become a monk:

> Whatever body, Rahula, whatever feeling, or perception, or mental formations, or consciousness, be it past, future or present, be it your own, or be it external to you, be it gross or subtle, mean or noble, remote or near, if you see it all so: --"This is not mine, I am not it, it is not my self"--thus seeing by right insight the thing as it really is, you are liberated, without grasping (S: XVII, 2, 22).

Understanding our nature by "right insight" is more than just an intellectual exercise. It is easy to think and even believe that we are not our bodies, but to abandon the conceit of "mine" and "my" requires a training and a practice in morality and concentration. A person might think that he is not his body, and feel fully convinced, but yet be upset when he overhears someone saying that he does not look good or his body is an unattractive size or shape. Or he might feel pleased or even proud if someone says his body looks good. These responses to hearing either criticism or praise of the body reveal identification with the body. We could easily generate similar examples involving the intellect and how "smart" or "stupid" one is. The point is that our identifications with some of the aggregates is subtle and deeply rooted. Unearthing and letting go of whatever identities we have with one or more of the aggregates is an essential step on the path to liberation.

While essential as a tool for liberation, anatta is also a practical tool on a more mundane level, as the following story illustrates (S: XXII, I, 1). During a visit with the Buddha, the elderly layman Nakulapitar tells the Buddha that he is "a broken-down old man, aged, far-gone in years... sick and always ailing." He asks the Buddha for "cheer and comfort."

To deal with the suffering of his body, the Buddha tells Nakulapitar to train himself: "Though my body is sick, my mind shall not be sick." The layman Nakulapitar reports this conversation to the venerable Sariputta who asks him whether he had asked the Buddha how he should train himself about how the body can be sick and the mind not sick. Nakulapitar tells Sariputta he did not ask the Buddha and so he asks Sariputta instead. Sariputta answers that the person trained in this way does not regard

> body as the self, regards not the self as having body, nor body as being in the self, nor self as being in body. He does not say 'I am body,' he does not say 'body is mine,' nor is he possessed by this idea. As he is not possessed with these ideas, when body alters and changes owing to the unstable and changeful nature of body, then sorrow and grief, woe, lamentation, and despair do not arise in him (S: iii, 4-5).

In short, says Sariputta, that is how the body can be sick but not the mind. He sees that none of the aggregates is himself.

When we no longer identify with any of the five aggregates, there is no foundation for a sense of the personal, for the notions of "I am" and "me" and "mine" are dependent on these five aggregates (S: XII, 4, 1). Nonetheless, the persistence of a sense of self may leave us with the lingering question: Is there anything beyond these five aggregates that is truly me?

This question misses the point of the personal being dependent on the five aggregates. If one removes the aggregates, what is there that could possibly be personal? What makes me the person I am involves my body, my feelings, my memory, and my volitional impulses. If all of that is gone, what remains that could ground the personal? Consider the following dialogue between the Buddha and the Wanderer Vacchagotta:

"But, Master Gotama, the monk whose mind is thus released: Where does he reappear?"

"'Reappear,' Vaccha, does not apply ...."

"In that case, Venerable Gotama, he does not reappear.

"'Does not reappear', Vaccha, does not apply."

"... both does and does not reappear"

"...does not apply"

"... neither does nor does not reappear."

"...does not apply."

"...At this point, Master Gotama, I am befuddled; at this point, confused...."

"Of course you're befuddled, Vaccha. Of course you're confused. Deep, Vaccha, is this phenomenon... beyond the scope of conjecture, subtle, to-be-experienced by the wise.... That being the case, I will now put some questions to you. Answer as you see fit. How do you construe this, Vaccha: If a fire were burning in front of you, would you know that, 'This fire is burning in front of me'?"

"...yes..."

"And suppose some one were to ask you, Vaccha, 'This fire burning in front of you, dependent on what is it burning?"

"... I would reply, 'This fire burning in front of me is burning dependent on grass and timber as its sustenance."

"If the fire burning in front of you were to go out, would you know that,'This fire burning in front of me has gone out'?"

"...yes..."

"And suppose someone were to ask you, 'This fire that has gone out in front of you, in which direction from here has it gone? East? West? North? Or South?' Thus asked, how would you reply?"

"That does not apply, Master Gotama. Any fire dependent on a sustenance of grass and timber, being unnourished--from having consumed that sustenance...--is classified simply as 'out'."

"Even so, Vaccha, any physical form ... feeling... perception... mental process... any act of consciousness by which one describing the Tathagata[3] would describe him: That the Tathagata has abandoned, its root destroyed, like an uprooted palm tree, deprived of the conditions of existence, not destined for future arising.... Freed from the classification of consciousness, Vaccha, the Tathagata is deep, boundless, hard to fathom, like the sea" (M: 72, 16-20).

Like a sentence that might say which direction the fire went after it went out, some sentences attempt to say what literally is nonsensical. Certain things cannot be said because they "do not apply." When the answers would have no meaning, the Buddha does not try to answer the questions. In these discussions the Buddha predates the widely respected twentieth century philosopher Ludwig Wittgenstein, who wrote:

> If the answer cannot be put into words, the question, too, cannot be put into words. The *riddle* does not exist. If a question can be put at all, then it can also be answered.[4]

Wittgenstein is not saying that, for a riddle not to exist, we need to be unable to utter or write the words of the question. Rather, he is saying that, when we use words to ask what lacks a meaningful answer, there is no riddle.

Just as the Buddha's teachings did not resolve Vacchagotta's questions, so too these comments might not resolve the reader's. One might still feel that more that can be said. The Buddha did say, did he not, that "the Tathagata is deep, boundless, hard to fathom, like the sea"?

The Buddha as Ineffabilist

As we saw in the Buddha's conversations with Malunkyaputta and Vacchagotta, the Buddha gave different reasons on different occasions for putting aside metaphysical questions. In talking with Ananda after a visit from Vacchagotta, the Buddha provides yet another reason for not answering such questions. Vacchagotta the Wanderer asked the Buddha:

> "Now, master Gotama, is there a self?"
> At these words the Exalted One was silent.
> "How, then, master Gotama, is there not a self?"
> For a second time also the Exalted One was silent.
> Then Vacchagotta the Wanderer rose from his seat and went away.
> Now not long after the departure of the Wanderer, the venerable Ananda said to the Exalted One:
> "How is it, lord, that the Exalted One gave no answer... ?"
> "If, Ananda, when asked by the Wanderer: 'Is there a self?' I had replied to him: 'There is a self,' then, Ananda, that would be siding with the recluses and brahmins who are eternalists. But if, Ananda, when asked: 'Is there not a self?' I had replied that it does not exist,

that, Ananda, would be siding with those recluses and brahmins who are annihilationists. Again, Ananda, when asked by the Wanderer: 'Is there a self?' had I replied that there is, would my reply be in accordance with the knowledge that all things are not-self?"

"Surely not, lord."

"Again, Ananda, when asked by Vacchagotta the Wanderer: 'Is there not a self?' had I replied that there is not, it would have been more bewilderment for the bewildered Vacchagotta. For he would have said: 'Formerly indeed I had a self, but now I have not one anymore'" (S: XLIV, X, 10).

The first reasons the Buddha says he remained is because answering either question would have committed him to eternalism or annihilationism, two metaphysical views debated in his time. These unending debates did not lead to liberation and the Buddha taught the Middle Way between these two extremes. In addition, the Buddha offers two other reasons why he did not answer Vacchagotta's questions. One is that no thing, phenomenon, or condition is the self. The other is that, since the Buddha had prior conversations with Vacchagotta and knew how Vacchagotta was liable to become confused, he did not want to confuse Vacchagotta any farther.

The Buddha's reluctance to answer this and other metaphysical questions led some of his contemporaries, and some of ours,[5] to claim that the Buddha was agnostic on these questions. The Buddha denied being agnostic and never said that the ultimate nature of reality was unknowable to him, only that nothing useful or meaningful can be said. If we reflect on the fact that the ultimate nature of things is beyond the conditioned realm, we see the plausibility of the Buddha's reluctance to say anything. Since all our language refers to the conditioned world, anything that might be said about what was not part of the conditioned world would have to be said in the language of conditioned phenomena. Trying to describe or convey in language any positive content about Nibbana or the ultimate nature of awareness would for that reason only be misleading. Nibbana is beyond the conditioned world or else there could be no release from suffering. The Buddha did clearly point to the unconditioned, but did so in negative terms, denying that properties of conditioned phenomena apply to the unconditioned. Even the name of the unconditioned, "not" "conditioned," is a negative term. When it comes to describing Nibbana or any other transcendent reality in positive terms, the Buddha was silent.[6] He was an ineffabilist.

The Buddha remained an ineffabilist for his forty-five years of teaching. During that period he frequently said that all he taught was suffering and the release from suffering. He steadfastly refrained from answering any of the metaphysical questions he was frequently asked. Consider another exchange, this time initiated by a visiting king:

> "Pray, lord, does the Tathagata exist after death?"
> "Not revealed by me, great king, is this matter."
> "Then, lord, the Tathagata does not exist after death."
> "That also, great king, is not revealed by me."
> ".... does the Tathagata both exist and not exist after death?"
> "That also, great king, is not revealed by me."
> "Then, lord, the Tathagata neither exists nor not-exists after death."
> "That also, great king, is not revealed by me."

At the end of the discussion, the Buddha says to the king:

> "If one should try to define the Tathagata by his bodily form, that bodily form of the Tathagata is abandoned.... Set free from reckoning as body, great king, is the Tathagata. He is deep, boundless, unfathomable, just like the mighty ocean. To say, 'The Tathagata exists after death,' does not apply. To say, 'The Tathagata exists not after death,' does not apply. To say, 'The Tathagata both exists and does not, neither exists nor not-exists after death,' does not apply" (S: XLIV, X, 1).

The student of philosophy will recognize in the conversations of the Buddha with Malunkyaputta, Vacchagotta, and the king a clarity and precision of speech that illustrates what Ludwig Wittgenstein described as the only correct method in philosophy:

> The right method in philosophy would be to say nothing except what can be said using sentences such as those of natural science-- which of course has nothing to do with philosophy--and then, to show those wishing to say something metaphysical that they failed to give any meaning to certain signs in their sentences. Although they would not be satisfied--they would feel you weren't teaching them any philosophy--*this* would be the only right method.[7]

29

Wittgenstein ends the book from which the above quote is drawn with the statement: "What we cannot speak about we must pass over in silence." For the Buddha, anatta is a reflection on all that we can experience, on all about which we can speak. It is a tool a person may use in search of truth and insight. Every phenomenon that one notices, every thing or title or position or process with which one might identify or in terms of which one thinks of himself, each is anatta. A feeling, the process of thinking, the body, a vocation, an occupation--each is not me, not mine, and I am not it. Beyond that, the Buddha is silent.[8]

What Can Be Said

The Four Noble Truths refer to phenomena and to the causal factors that lead to suffering. The scope of these four statements includes all conditioned phenomena. When listeners pressed the Buddha on metaphysical questions, he oftentimes pointed out that all he taught was suffering and the way out of suffering (M: 22. 38). On some occasions, however, the Buddha described a causal relationship among conditioned phenomena beginning with ignorance and ending with suffering. The following was one such occasion.

The wanderer Kassapa approached the Buddha and interrupted his alms rounds to ask whether one's suffering is caused by oneself, caused by another, caused both by oneself and another, or caused neither by oneself nor by another but by chance. The Buddha said that each of these alternatives was false. Kassapa then asked if suffering was nonexistent. When the Buddha said that "suffering is," Kassapa continued, "then Master Gotama neither knows nor sees suffering"(S: XII, 2, 17). When the Buddha responded that he does know the nature of suffering and that he is one who sees suffering, Kassapa asked him to teach the nature of suffering.

The Buddha first addressed Kassapa's first two questions, saying that a person who believes that his suffering is caused by himself holds a version of the eternalist view, for he believes that he is a person who exists from moment to moment and so both causes and experiences his own suffering. A person who believes that his suffering is caused by another holds the annihilationist view, for he believes that the person who causes suffering and the person who experiences it are never the same. Rather than embracing either of these extremes,[9] the Buddha taught dependent origination:

> Ignorance conditions volitional impulses; volitional impulses condition consciousness; consciousness conditions body and mind;

body and mind condition the six senses; the six senses condition sense contact; sense contact conditions feeling; feeling conditions craving; craving conditions clinging; clinging conditions becoming; becoming conditions birth; birth conditions aging and death, sorrow, lamentation, pain, grief and despair. Thus arises the whole mass of suffering.

The reason this teaching is called "dependent origination" is that the origin of each component is dependent on the component that precedes it and is a determinant of the component that follows it.

We have, until now, emphasized in our discussion the conditions that begin with desire (craving) and end with suffering (sorrow, lamentation, pain, grief and despair). With the teaching of dependent origination, the Buddha pointed out that these conditions can be traced back to ignorance: positive feelings are a determinant of desire; sense contact is a determinant of feelings; and, eventually, all the way back to ignorance.

The teaching of dependent origination also involved the causal factors leading from the cessation of ignorance to the cessation of suffering:

> With the complete fading away and cessation of ignorance, volitional impulses cease. With the cessation of volitional impulses, consciousness ceases. With the cessation of consciousness, body and mind cease. With the cessation of body and mind . . . pain, grief and despair cease. This is the cessation to the whole mass of suffering.

The English word 'cessation' does not accurately capture the meaning of the word 'nirodha' which it translates. Even those who see the shortfalls of this translation have continued to use the word 'cessation' in order not to cause confusion for those who know the texts and because there is no single word in English that captures what is meant.[10] Following P.A. Payutto,[11] either of the following might more accurately render the meaning:

> Being free of ignorance, there is freedom from volitional impulses. Being free of volitional impulses, there is freedom from consciousness . . .

or

> When ignorance is no longer a problem, volitional impulses are no longer a problem. When volitional impulses are no longer a problem, consciousness is no longer a problem . . . .

31

Each of these renditions better expresses a middle path that does not require annihilation for liberation from suffering. Each better reflects the three aspects of the Second Noble Truth which requires the abandoning and letting go of desire, not the annihilation of desire.

Like everything the Buddha taught, the causal relationships among the factors mentioned in dependent origination are intended to be a reflection on experience and so recognizable in experience. We know from experience that positive feelings can lead to desire. Likewise, once we begin clinging to anything--our ability to do something, to be in a certain relationship, to be in a particular public role--we can experience a sense of identity as we come to see ourselves as a carpenter, spouse, student, or teacher. In these ways clinging leads to a sense of becoming (a carpenter, a spouse, a student, a teacher), which is a birth, and that which is born (carpenter, spouse, student, teacher) will eventually have a cessation.

Dependent origination is a principle of cause and effect. It is a lawlike causal relationship among conditions and does not depend on anyone being aware of it. It is part of what can be said. On several occasions the Buddha taught dependent origination as the Middle Way between metaphysical extremes.[12] Dependent origination, however, is not the path out of suffering.[13] The Buddha's teaching of the way out of suffering is the Fourth Noble Truth. To that we now turn.

----

1. The criteria of personal identity are found among the five aggregates. In contemporary Western philosophy the dispute is between those who defend bodily identity as the criterion of personal identity, and those who defend memory as the criterion of personal identity. See Derek Parfit, *Reasons and Persons* (Oxford: Clarendon Press, 1984), pp.199-306.

2. David Hume, *A Treatise of Human Nature* (Clarendon Press, Oxford: 1960), p. 253 [first published, 1739]. For a comparion of the Buddha's account of the self and Hume's, see Pliny Nolan Jacobson, *Buddhism: The Religion of Analysis* (Carbondale and Edwardsville: Southern Illinois University Press, 1966).

3. The word 'Tathagata' refers to one 'one who has truly gone' and the Buddha often uses this term to refer to himself.

4. Ludwig Wittgenstein, *Wittgenstein's Tractatus*, trans. by Daniel Kolak (Mountain View, CA: Mayfield Publishing Company, 1998), 6.5.

5. E.A. Burtt, "The Contribution of Buddhism to Philosophic Thought," in *Knowledge and Conduct* (Buddhist Publication Society, Andy, Ceylon, 1963), pp. 46-50.

6. There are gentle crosscurrents in the texts on this point. At AN: 10.60, Nibbana is described as peaceful, although the other descriptions are negations expressed as relinquishments and exhaustions. At SN: xliii , forty-four names of Nibbana occur, most of which are negations and it is unclear that any would be able to convey the content of Nibbana in words to those who never had the insight (even the word 'peace' refers to aspects of the conditioned).

7. Op. cit., 6.53.

8. But see note 6 above.

9. See also SN: ii, 16.

10. One problem with the standard translation is the implication that the Buddha, after his enlightenment and while he was alive, was not free from ignorance because sense contact had not ceased. Translating 'nirodha' in the way P.A. Payutto suggests below solves this problem: the Buddha is enlightened, sense contact still occurs, but it is no longer a problem.

11. P.A. Payutto, *Dependent Origination: The Buddhist Law of Conditionality* (Buddhadamma Foundaton, Bangkok: 1994), esp. pp. 106-108. Also see Vsm, XVI, 18.

12. See, for example, S: XII, 2, 15; S: XII, 2, 18; S: XII, 2, 19 where the extremes are eternalism and annihilationism. At S: XII, 5, 48 the the extremes are the four "worldly wisdoms": everything is, nothing is, everything is one, everything is a plurality.

13. For a thorough discussion of this point see Payutto, ibid., pp. 86-90.

5

Wisdom

The wisdom component of the Eightfold path has two parts: understanding and attitude. From the Buddha's perspective, wisdom is not completely cognitive or cerebral but involves character traits that include equanimity, and this more closely agrees with what we ordinarily mean by "wisdom" than a purely cerebral notion. If we imagine what a wise person would be like, we would likely describe a person who not only has a depth of knowledge, but also a person who in difficult circumstances remains poised and calm. These components of wisdom are included in Right Attitude, the second part of the wisdom component.

Right Understanding

Right Understanding is the complete understanding of things as they are. Since Right Understanding encompasses the whole of the teachings and is the culmination of the practice, we might expect it to be the last item of the Eightfold Path. Yet each element of the Path is to be developed, this development occurs in degrees, and each supports the others. With Right Understanding at the head of the list we begin with the aim of the path as a guide for developing the other components of the path (M: 117, 10-34).

There is a saying that a person who has not realized his metaphysics is like an ox carrying a load of books. In Buddhism the aim of the practice is to realize directly the truth about how things are. As Right Understanding matures, it involves direct realization and excludes beliefs, wishes, or speculations. The following exchange makes this clear:

> The wanderer Vacchagotta went to the Blessed One and exchanged greetings with him. When this courteous and amiable talk was finished, he sat down at one side and asked the Blessed One: "...does Master Gotama hold the view: 'The world is eternal: only this is true, anything otherwise is worthless'?"
>
> "Vaccha, I do not hold this view...."
>
> [Similar questions and answers follow about: 'The world is not eternal'; 'The world is finite'; 'The world is infinite'; 'The soul and the body are the same'; 'The soul is one thing and the body another'; 'After death a Tathagata exists'; 'After death a Tathagata does not exist'; 'After death a Tathagata both exists and does not exist'; 'After death a Tathagata neither exists nor does not exist'.]
>
> "How is it then, Master Gotama? When Master Gotama is asked each of these ten questions, hr replies: 'I do not hold that view.' What danger does Master Gotama see that he does not take up any of these speculative views?"
>
> "Vaccha, the position that the world is eternal is a thicket of views, a wilderness of views, a contortion of views, a vacillation of views, a fetter of views. It is beset by suffering, by vexation . . . and it does not lead to disenchantment, to dispassion, to cessation, to peace, to direct knowledge, to enlightenment, to Nibbana.... Seeing this danger, I do not take up any of these speculative views."
>
> "Then does Master Gotama hold any speculative view at all?"
>
> "Vaccha, 'speculative view' is something that the Tathagata has put away. For the Tathagata, Vaccha, has seen with direct vision[1]: 'Such is material form, such its origin, such its disappearance... feeling...perception... mental formations... consciousness.... Therefore, I say, with the destruction, fading away, cessation, giving up, and relinquishing of all conceivings, all excogitations, all I-making, mine-making, and the underlying tendency to conceit, the Tathagata is liberated through not clinging." (M: 72.1-15.)

The Buddha tells us that on matters of a metaphysical nature, he is beyond views. Instead, he has "direct vision" of the nature of the origin and cessation of the aggregates. This direct knowing is the maturation of Right Understanding that includes understanding things as they are: impermanent (anicca), unable to satisfy ultimately (dukkha), and not-self (anatta).

As our awareness of these three characteristics deepens, we notice that they are interrelated. That a phenomenon is impermanent often leads to its being unsatisfactory. On the other hand, when we realize the impermanence of a phenomenon, we tend not to become attached to it lasting and thereby tend not to suffer when it ceases. For example, we do not become attached to the fragrance of cherry blossoms as we walk under a grove of cherry trees or become attached to the beauty of the sky as the sun sets. Furthermore, our memory of the fragrance of the cherry blossoms or of the beauty of the sunset do not bring up a sense of loss or grief for those phenomena. The feat required of us is to extend this wisdom to everything that is impermanent.

Right Attitude

The Buddha defines Right Attitude as the thought of renunciation, the thought of non-ill-will, the thought of harmlessness (D: 22.21). The Pali word translated as 'thought', however, is much more dynamic and has an intentional aspect. For this reason translators and commentators refer to the second component of the Eightfold Path as Right Intention, Right Aspiration, Right Motive, or, as we do here, Right Attitude.

The Twin Verses

The opening verses of the Dhammapada clearly state the centrality of thought and attitude on our own lives:

> All that we are is the result of what we have thought: it is founded on our thoughts, it is made up of our thoughts. If a man speaks or acts with an evil thought, pain follows him, as the wheel follows the foot of the ox that draws the carriage.
> All that we are is the result of what we have thought: it is founded on our thoughts, it is made up of our thoughts. If a man speaks or acts with a pure thought, happiness follows him, like a shadow that never leaves him.
> "He abused me, he beat me, he defeated me, he robbed me"--in those who harbor such thoughts hatred will never cease.
> "He abused me, he beat me, he defeated me, he robbed me"--in those who do not harbor such thoughts hatred will cease.
> For hatred does not cease by hatred at any time; hatred ceases by love--this is an eternal law (Dhp. 1-5).

The first two verses of the Dhammapada, referred to as the "twin verses," state that what happens to us is a direct result of our thoughts and attitudes. The text emphasizes that this is an unavoidable feature of life by using similes about ox carts and shadows. For us who often work indoors and travel about in motorized vehicles, these similes do not carry the weight they did at the time of the Buddha. Their significance is to bring home the inevitability of the relationship between our thoughts and how life is for us.

These reflections on the ill effects of evil thoughts or the good effects of good thoughts may seem like hocus-pocus. The following example illustrates that these reflections are plausible. Suppose Mary is angry with someone she thinks of as her enemy. She is likely to experience moments of feeling upset, annoyed, or perhaps furious, and those attitudes automatically color her world and occupy her mind. The result is Mary may not be free to enjoy an entire evening, since she will spend some time thinking and feeling anger toward her enemy. Likewise, if Mary were to find herself near her enemy's residence, she may well not be as able to enjoy the lutelike song of the thrush. In these ways Mary's hateful thoughts and anger make her world less pleasant. Of course, Mary may also want to retaliate against her enemy, and, if she does, this person, in turn, may want to counter Mary's act of retaliation. This is how feuds begin and there is no way to end them by delivering a final blow that evens up the score. No party to a feud, or their friends, or their progeny, will perceive the last blow against them as the blow that sets the record straight. Hatred ceases only when we let go of hateful thoughts and attitudes. Notice that if Mary acts out her hatred but the person she acts against never reciprocates, nonetheless Mary will plausibly experience additional tension as she awaits retaliation.

On the other hand, suppose, instead, a different person named Alice who thinks of no one as an enemy. She will not be upset by moments of ill-will, thoughts of vengeance, or involved in plotting acts of retaliation. It is plausible that Alice's world is happier and more peaceful than Mary's because she lives free from thoughts of hatred and ill-will.[2]

There is enough substance in the twin verses and the passages immediately following to ground a full account of why nonviolence is both good for the individual and the only way to create a society in which there is a stable foundation for the flourishing of all. That discussion must be pursued elsewhere. Here we turn to four specific attitudes that play a major role in the practice of Theravada Buddhism.

Lovingkindness, compassion, sympathetic joy, and equanimity

Lovingkindness (metta) is the first of the four boundless states that are to be developed by the practicing Buddhist. The practice of lovingkindness involves developing the attitude: "May all beings. . . be free from enmity, free from affliction and anxiety, and live happily" (Vsm: IX, 52). The Pali word 'metta' is often translated as 'lovingkindness' and sometimes as 'goodwill', although, where possible we will simply use the Pali word 'metta'.

In developing the attitude of compassion (karuna), the second of the four boundless states, one develops the attitude that all beings be free from suffering. The third state is sympathetic joy (mudita): being joyful at the good fortune of others. As much as metta and compassion are underdeveloped in modern life, sympathetic joy is antithetical to the competitive mode of schooling, business, and athletics that are common today. The final trait, equanimity (upekkha), does not imply indifference, an unfortunate translation that appeared at the beginning of the twentieth century, but rather "equal" (equa-) "spirit" (animus) under all circumstances. We intuitively expect a person of wisdom to have equanimity.

In the early texts of Theravada Buddhism the emphasis on metta, compassion, sympathetic joy, and equanimity often has a meditative focus:

> With his heart filled with loving-kindness, he dwells intent pervading one quarter, the second, the third, the fourth. Thus he dwells pervading the whole world, upwards, downwards, across, everywhere, always with a heart filled with loving-kindness, abundant, unbounded, without hate or ill-will . . . Then with his heart filled with compassion, . . . with sympathetic joy, . . . with equanimity, . . . he dwells pervading the whole world, upwards, downwards, across, everywhere, always with a heart filled with equanimity, abundant, unbounded, without hate or ill-will. . . . By this meditation, Vasettha, by this liberation of the heart through compassion . . . through sympathetic joy . . . through equanimity, he leaves nothing untouched, nothing unaffected in the sensuous sphere (D: I, 252).

The development of metta requires patience and the abandoning of all hatred and aversions. It is developed first by using oneself as the object, then a person towards whom one feels neutral, then a person towards whom one feels positive, and then, if there are any, a person whom one considers an enemy or towards whom one has some negative feelings (Vsm: IX, 3-43). The practice of metta supports us in abandoning ill-will towards others (Ud. IV, 1) and makes us more peaceful and more serene (Vsm: IX, 59-76). In addition, metta supports us in being non-judgemental, open and patient with all phenomena that may arise within ourselves, thus allowing us to investigate them without aversion. The texts characterize metta as a condition that helps liberate the mind from barriers, leading to an impartiality toward all beings.[3] Metta understood in this way is not a gushy sentimentality but involves the complete abandonment of aversion, hatred, ill-will, fear, repression, discrimination, and all those tendencies that cause us to reject people and situations.

While metta clearly has a powerful meditative function and undermines our ill-will towards others, limiting our understanding of compassion to meditative practice would be an incomplete understanding of its role in the Buddha's teachings. The development of compassion also influences action, and it does so in two ways. The first is non-cruelty. As Buddhaghosa also notes, "it is not possible to practice compassion and be cruel to breathing things simultaneously"(Vsm: IX, 99). The second influence of compassion involves allaying suffering and making cruelty subside (Vsm: IX, 94).

The Buddha was an exemplar of compassion, for he did what he could to allay the suffering of all human beings.

> Whatever, Ananda, is to be done out of compassion by a teacher seeking the welfare of his disciples and compassionate for them, that has been done by me for you (M: III:302).

Out of compassion the Buddha taught the Dhamma, performing the external actions of teaching. But he also responded compassionately to people in more subtle ways, as the following story illustrates.

A young woman, named Gotami (no relation to the Buddha), was out of her mind with grief for her young dead son. She took her son on her hip and went from house to house looking for medicine. Most people made fun of her, but one man, understanding her grief, told her that the Buddha alone would know the right medicine for her son.

So she went to the Buddha. The Buddha did not laugh at her or tell her that her son was dead or make any pronouncements about impermanence. Instead, he told her that she did well in coming to him for medicine. "Go enter the city," he instructed her, "make the rounds of the entire city, beginning at the beginning, and in whatever house no one has ever died, from that house fetch tiny grains of mustard seed."

She did as she was told. At every house, when the people offered grains of mustard seed, she asked if anyone had died, and they told her about the dead. In this manner she went from house to house but was unable to collect any mustard seeds. In every house someone had died.

Realizing that the Buddha out of compassion had wanted her to see this for herself, she took her son to the burning-ground and said good-bye to him. "Dear little son," she said to him as she held him in her arms. "I thought that you alone had been overtaken by this thing which men call death. But you are not the only one death has overtaken. This is a law common to all mankind." Then she sought out the Buddha. When he asked her if she had gotten the tiny grains of mustard seed, she told him that she was finished with the business of medicine for her son and asked to go to him for refuge.[4]

----

1. See note 720, p. 1274, of the translation cited in the abbreviation section by Bhikkhu Nanamoli and Bhikkhu Bodhi

2. Isn't this part of what Wittgenstein meant when he wrote the following? "If the good or bad exercise of the will does alter the world, it can alter only the limits of the world, not the facts--not what can be expressed by means of language. In short the effect must be that it becomes an altogether different world. It must, so to speak, wax and wane as a whole. The world of the happy man is a different one from that of the unhappy man." See Ludwig Wittgenstein, *Tractatus Logico-Philosophicus*, trans. By D. F. Pears and B. F. McGuinness (London: Routledge & Kegan Paul, 1963), 6.43.

3. The characteristic of a mature metta practice is an impartiality that is kindly towards all. The following story is meant to illustrate the degree of impartiality achieved by the practice of metta. Bandits come upon a group of four monks and ask one of the monks to choose a monk that the bandits can kill for a human sacrifice. Among the other three monks is a friend, a neutral person, and a hostile person. The monk who is to choose is developed in metta and so chooses none of the other three monks nor himself. Instead, "he does not see a single one among the four people to be given to the bandits and he directs his mind impartially towards himself and towards these three [other] people" (Vsm. IX, 41).

4. From the Anguttara Commentary : 225-227.

6

Morality

There is a tendency among those who are attracted to Buddhism to sidestep morality and focus on meditation. The widely respected Cambodian monk, the Venerable Mahaghosananda, points out that focusing only on meditation is like trying to walk using only one leg. The other great support for maturation on the Buddha's path is the practice of morality. When the Buddha gave his first sermon he gave as much emphasis to the moral components as he did to the meditative components. Each is necessary to solve the problem of suffering.

Thinking of the meditative elements and the moral elements of the Eightfold Path as independent reflects the Western philosophical orthodoxy of separating epistemological issues from ethical ones. The Buddha did not make this separation. According to the Buddha, to know things as they are, one has to live in an appropriate way.

The Preliminary Step

There is an old adage, "birds of a feather flock together." The meaning of this adage is that people who are alike in their habits, their aims, and patterns of behavior befriend each other. The same is true for those interested in following the Buddha's path. If a person is thinking about beginning to practice what the Buddha taught, these practices are alien to the contemporary ideology of competition, accumulation, and instant gratification. Since friends and acquaintances influence us tremendously, it is important for someone interested in the Eightfold Path to associate with people who have similar aspirations.

For the person who is beginning on the path, the Buddha emphasized the importance of having "noble friends and noble companions." The Buddha tells us that "when the heart's release is immature this [noble friends] is the first thing that conduces to its maturity" (Ud. IV, I).[1] It is relevant to note that the Buddha spent much effort creating a community of monks and nuns who would not only transmit his teachings to future generations, but who would support each other and laypersons in their practice.

Right Speech

The first of the moral components of the Eightfold Path is Right Speech. Right Speech involves not only not lying, but also not gossiping, not slandering, and not speaking harshly. The Buddha says:

> And what, monks, is Right Speech? Refraining from lying, refraining from slander, refraining from harsh speech, refraining from frivolous speech. This is called Right Speech. (M: 22, 21)

A person initially reading about the moral guidelines and, specifically, Right Speech, may wonder what any of this has to do with suffering. The answer is that to be free of suffering we need to be free of desire and attachment, each of which we tend to reinforce with wrong speech. Imagine a person lies to her husband about where she spent the early part of the evening. Suppose she was flirting with someone else but tells her husband that she was working late. Why would she lie? One possibility is that she feels remorse for what she did and does not want to hurt her partner. Although this may be her motivation, it is at least as plausible that she lies to protect her self-interest--to avoid the hassle of a heated discussion, the inconvenience of not getting a good night's sleep, or the distress of having her spouse leave. Insofar as self-interest is her motivation, she lies to protect her interests and desires. Lying in this and other instances is an attempt to control the other person. Typically, the reason we want to control another person is to satisfy our own desires.

If we think about why we gossip, or slander, or even speak harshly, our motivation typically is to promote our own ends at the expense of others. In these cases of wrong speech, we are reinforcing the very desires we are trying to abandon. If our purpose is to be liberated from suffering, we will try to abandon rather than reinforce our desires and attachments that are the cause of our suffering. Right Speech is one way to begin.

Right Action

Right Action, the second component of the moral section of the Eightfold Path, includes refraining from killing, refraining from taking what is not given, and refraining from sexual misconduct. The Buddha says:

> And what, monks, is Right Action? Refraining from taking life, refraining from taking what is not given, refraining from sexual misconduct. This is called Right Action. (M: 22,21)

To refrain from killing does not require that we not kill anything, but only that we not intentionally kill any sentient being (beings that can experience pain and suffering). Intention plays a major role in Buddhist ethics. If an action is performed unintentionally, it is not a violation of Right Action. For example, if I inadvertently brush up against an ant while going through a doorway and kill it, that is not a violation of the restraint on killing. To kill a sentient being intentionally is a different matter. When we kill intentionally, we typically are putting our own desires ahead of the desires of the sentient beings we kill. If this is what we are doing, we are reinforcing desire and a sense of "me" and "mine." An intention to kill, typically, is rooted in one of the three sources of the unwholesome: greed, hatred, or delusion. It is for this reason that intention is critical. By acting on an intention that is rooted in the unwholesome, rather than abandoning these unwholesome roots and related attachments, we are only reinforcing them.

To refrain from taking what has not been given involves refraining from stealing and any other actions that involve taking what is not given. Precisely what other actions in addition to stealing constitute taking what is not given will depend not only on local rules and customs, but also on one's own growth and understanding of this practical restraint. For instance, when, if ever, is borrowing without asking an action of taking what is not given? Since taking what is not given typically involves putting our desires ahead of the desires of the owner of the object taken, this act too not only reinforces greed, but also the delusion of "me" and "mine."

Sexual misconduct refers to sexual conduct that involves manipulation, deception, out-and-out lying, and any sexual conduct that might harm one's sexual partner. While rape and child molestation clearly involve harm and coercion, and adultery often involves lying or promise-breaking, many types of sexual misconduct depend on manipulation. Lying is one way of manipulating, but so is taking advantage of another person's vulnerabilities. For example, assume that an admirer would not wish for a sexual encounter with a physically beautiful seducer if he understood, as well as the seducer does, the utter improbability of a long term relationship. Suppose the seducer tells her admirer that there is absolutely no chance a long term relationship will evolve out of a sexual encounter while knowing that the admirer is so caught up in wanting such a relationship that her explicit denial will not be convincing. For the seducer to engage in sex with such an admirer under these conditions would not seem to be part of Right Action. This example illustrates the general point that violations of these restraints, called precepts in Buddhism, tend to have the dynamic that one person is taking advantage of another.

Reflection and the precepts

From the Buddha's perspective, the practice of Right Speech and Right Action requires reflection. The Buddha tells his son, the monk Rahula, to purify his actions of body, speech and mind "by repeatedly reflecting upon them"(M: I, 420). The Buddha encourages a reflection familiar to anyone who has thought about the morality of action: "does this action that I have done with the body lead to my own affliction, or the affliction of others, or to the affliction of both?"(M: I, 416) If it does, that is reason to restrain in the future. If it does not, "you can abide happy and glad, training day and night in wholesome states"(M: I, 417). To help us become clear how an action affects others, we are encouraged to develop an awareness of how things would be for us if the situation were reversed. The Buddha illustrates this reflective technique in the following passage:

> In this matter . . . the disciple thus reflects: Here am I, fond of my life, not wanting to die, fond of pleasure and averse from pain. Suppose someone should rob me of my life (fond of life as I am and not wanting to die, fond of pleasure and averse from pain), it would not be a thing pleasing or delightful to me. If I, in my turn, should rob of his life one fond of his life, not wanting to die. . . . For a state that is not pleasant or delightful to me must be so to him also: and a state that is not pleasing or delightful to me--how could I inflict that upon another? (S: LV, XI, I, vii)

The Buddha suggests similar reflections for theft, sexual misconduct, and wrong speech. Since we are like those with whom we interact, our acts will affect them in the same way as similar acts would affect us, and so we should act accordingly. This is the Buddha's version of the familiar Golden Rule: Do unto others as you would have them do unto you.

The texts suggest a second mode of reflection. After the Buddha identifies unwholesome acts as killing living beings, taking what is not given, sexual misconduct, wrong speech, and ill will, he asks:

> And what is the root of the unwholesome? Greed is a root of the unwholesome; hate is a root of the unwholesome; delusion is a root of the unwholesome (M: 9.5).

When we look at the actions that are contrary to the morality component of the Eightfold path, the Buddha refers to these as unwholesome bodily actions, unwholesome verbal actions, and wrong livelihood.

> And what do these unwholesome habits originate from? Their origin is stated: they should be said to originate from the mind. Which mind? Though mind is multiple, varied, and of different aspects, there is mind affected by lust, by hate, and by delusion. Unwholesome habits originate from this (M: 78. 10).

Coming to know the root causes of our actions may also illuminate their moral skillfulness, or moral unskillfulness. Whether an action proceeds from greed or from compassion is largely irrelevant in mainstream Western philosophy. This important feature of Buddhist ethics may also help resolve what otherwise would remain controversial.

For example, is it right to file a tax return that fails to disclose all earned income? One might argue that no one has consented to pay taxes, that taxation is state coercion and therefore theft, that taxes pay for weapons and other evils, and that, by lowering the amount of tax one has to pay, one is simply keeping the thief of state from taking more of one's earnings. On the other hand, public services require tax dollars and at least some of the expenditures of tax dollars support these and other worthy projects. One can imagine how these opening volleys over the moral assessment of failing to report all earned income on a tax form might lead to a protracted and inconclusive discussion. But when we bring into the discussion the typical motivation for failing to report all earned income, then the Buddha's emphasis on the unwholesomeness of acting from greed, hatred or delusion might help resolve this disagreement. It seems safe to assume that the typical motivation for failing to report taxable income is to keep as much money as possible for oneself, one's family, and one's projects. If that were the motive, and in discussions of failing to report all earned income on tax forms this is, plausibly, the typical motive, then the Buddha's focus on greed clarifies what might otherwise be controversial. Acting from greed does not lead to liberation, and where greed motivates an action, we need to suspect that it may be an action that we should avoid. In this illustration understanding not only the consequences of the action but also its motivation helps us to understand how to apply the precepts in our daily lives.[2]

Although this illustration might suggest that the point of understanding the motive of an action is to identify clearly those external acts from which we are to refrain, it is important to emphasize that this is not the main point. The point in the end is always on mindfulness, on inner awareness. According to the late Venerable Ajahn Chah, a renowned Thai meditation master in the Theravada tradition, one should "just use the standards of the practice to reflect on yourself inwardly."[3] Repressing urges that motivate us to act would not lead to mindfulness, for we would have driven the urges out of our awareness. Likewise, acting on these motives or urges would not provide an occasion for coming to be mindful of them. Restraint, falling between repression and expression, creates a region in which we can become mindful of how we are, and so is an aspect of the Middle Way.

Right Livelihood

The third component of the morality section of the Eightfold Path is Right Livelihood. Minimally, right livelihood involves ways of supporting oneself and one's family that do not involve violating any of the precepts. Again, the investigation of what constitutes Right Livelihood for an individual will depend, in part, on her development and sensitivities. The Buddha explicitly excludes five activities from Right Livelihood:

> Monks, five trades ought not to be engaged in by a lay-disciple. What five? Trade in weapons, trade in human beings, trade in flesh, trade in spirits and trade in poisons. Verily, monks, these five trades are not be engaged in by a lay-disciple. (AN: V, 177)

The commentary to this passage notes that trading in flesh includes breeding and selling pigs, deer, and other animals. Trading in flesh, in weapons and in poisons clearly encourages others to kill and so to violate the first precept. To encourage others to do what is contrary to their own wellbeing is to fail to practice loving-kindness and compassion towards these other persons.

Morality, Monastics, and Laity

Some writers cite the entire Eightfold Path as Buddhist morality, whereas others identify the *Vinaya* (the texts containing the rules for monks and nuns) as the core or at least a part of Buddhist morality. While it is puzzling to think of the entire Eightfold Path as constituting morality, the *Vinaya* does serve as the guide for the conduct of monastics. Given the central role of monasticism in Theravada Buddhism, we will briefly look at the scope and rationale for these rules before examining the corresponding conventions for lay people.

The Vinaya

The *Vinaya* is one of the three collections (the *Triple Basket* or *Tipitaka*) of the early texts of Theravada Buddhism. In addition to the *Vinaya*, we have the *Nikayas*, which record the general teachings of the Buddha, and the *Abhidhamma*, a collection of philosophical and psychological analyses based on these teachings. The *Vinaya* is primarily the source of the rules for monks and nuns, the explanations of these rules, and the events that occasioned the Buddha's laying down the rules for monks and nuns.

The principal rules in the *Vinaya* are catalogued in the *Patimokha* (part of the *Vinaya*), a list of 227 rules that monastics recite together fortnightly. Some of these rules make more specific for monastics elements already found in the morality component of the Eightfold Path. For example, sexual misconduct for monastics precludes sexual intercourse. Other rules are specifically relevant to a monastic way of life. For example, there are rules about clothing (no more than three robes), food (no food between midday and the following dawn), and money (not allowed). There are also rules for meetings and rules for resolving disputes within the monastic community.

The rule against sexual intercourse was the first rule the Buddha laid down and a monk who violates this rule is no longer a member of the community of monks. Violating one of three other rules also nullifies one's membership in the monastic community: to take what is not given, to kill a human being (or hire an assassin or cause someone to kill himself), and to lie about having attained superior spiritual states. The first three of these rules are in an inverse order to the three precepts under Right Action. A rationale for this inversion is that the Buddha wanted to safeguard monastic life. Since sexual abstinence is an essential aspect of what it means to be a monk or nun, a violation of this abstinence nullifies the person's monasticism.

Taking what is not given has a high priority because it undermines the alms mendacacy aspect of Buddhist monasticism. The Buddha established his community as a community of alms mendicants. As alms mendicants, bhikkhus are to live on what the lay community gives them: shelter, clothing, medicine and food. Alms mendicancy encourages a life of non-acquisition and insures the daily presence of mendicants among the laity. For a Buddhist monastic to take what is not given would violate this basic feature of Buddhist monasticism.

The rules in the *Vinaya* were developed over many years. Initially rules were not needed. The first monks were sufficiently mature that even the least developed among them were already far enough along the path that the Buddha said they were "bound for enlightenment" (Vin: iii, 10). When one of the senior monks first asked that the Buddha establish rules for monks, the Buddha refused, saying that he would lay down rules only after conditions causing defects arose in the community. Those conditions include: after the community attained long standing, full development, wealth, or the monks attained great learning (Vin: iii, 9-10).

When finally the Buddha did lay down the first rule, he said he would develop rules for ten reasons:

> For the excellence of the Order, for the comfort of the Order, for the restraint of evil-minded men, for the ease of well-behaved monks, for the restraint of the asavas [roots of suffering] belonging to the here and now, for the combating of the asavas belonging to other worlds, for the benefit of non-believers, for the increase in the number of believers, for establishing Dhamma indeed, for following the rules of restraint (Vin. iii, 21).

Many of the rules in the *Vinaya* originated after lay people saw a monk behaving inappropriately, told other monks, and these monks in turn told the Buddha. If the Buddha determined the behavior was truly inappropriate, he typically scolded the "foolish monk" and then laid down a rule prohibiting such behavior in the future.

These rules institutionalized a way of life that has continued since the time of the Buddha.[4] Lay communities have provided food, robes, lodging, and medicines to monks and nuns since the Buddha's time and giving these items is called dana. Dana is essential for the survival of Buddhist monasticism, provides an opportunity for lay people to interact with Buddhist monks and nuns, and provides an occasion for lay people to express generosity.

The Five Precepts . . .

The five precepts are the institutionalized code of conduct for lay people. In addition to the four precepts contained in Right Speech and Right Action, there is a fifth precept to refrain from intoxicants. When lay Buddhists formally take upon themselves training on the path, they take upon themselves the following five precepts:

1. I undertake the training to refrain from destroying living creatures.
2. I undertake the training to refrain from taking what is not given.
3. I undertake the training to refrain from sexual misconduct.
4. I undertake the training to refrain from wrong speech.
5. I undertake the training to refrain from intoxicants.

The undertaking of morality as a training is a very different approach to morality than the fire and brimstone approach common in the West. If a person does not follow a rule, she should examine whether not following the rule has taken her further away from liberation or brought her nearer to liberation. There is no external punishment or reward. Like training rules for athletes, to violate a rule is to risk not developing one's potential or, in this case, to slow or even reverse the gradual process that leads to liberation.

When we act contrary to the first four precepts, we typically are reinforcing our own desires and attachments and putting our own gratification before that of someone else. The fifth precept is supportive of the first four. The Buddha noted that intoxicants lead to carelessness (M: 123, 9). When intoxicated, we may more easily fail to restrain from killing, taking what is not given, sexual misconduct, and wrong speech. The restraint on intoxicants also has another rationale, since a common motivation for consuming intoxicants is to sooth and eventually blur the mind in order to avoid what is unpleasant or to try to enhance what is pleasant. Either way, consuming intoxicants diminishes our awareness of things as they are and reinforces delusions that do not move us toward liberation.

While taking upon oneself the training in the five precepts puts a focus on external actions, the point of this training and the corresponding restraints is to become liberated from greed, anger and delusion. One does not do this simply by external restraint. "Not nakedness, not plaited hair, not dirt, not fasting, or lying on the earth; not rubbing with dust, not sitting motionless, can purify a mortal who has not overcome desires" (Dhp. 141). Following the five precepts as part of a training leading to liberation requires more than just restraining action: it requires that one be mindful. The focus is always: "Be not thoughtless, watch your thoughts" (Dhp: 327). Restraint creates the occasion for mindfulness to investigate feelings, thoughts, and motivations.

. . . and the Three Refuges

Lay Buddhists, in addition to taking the five precepts, traditionally take refuge in the Buddha, the Dhamma, and the Sangha. These are called the Triple Gem or the Three Refuges. In the contemporary world people seem to place their trust and find their security in power, insurance policies, and accumulations. Since we already have the habit of mind that leads us to take refuge, at issue is whether we want to modify our refuges in a way that might move us toward liberation.

One traditional understanding of the Three Refuges involves taking refuge as a commitment to the Triple Gem as guiding ideals for our lives. When we take refuge in the Buddha, on this account,[5] we take the Buddha as the supreme embodiment of purity, wisdom, and impeccability in conduct and understanding. We rely on him because he embodies these attainments. When we take refuge in the Dhamma, we take refuge in the teachings and the goal of the teachings: the unconditioned, nibbana. When we take refuge in the Sangha we take refuge in those persons of spiritual accomplishment who have realized the essential meaning of the Buddha's teachings for themselves. According to this account, it is only taking refuge in the Dhamma as nibbana that is a refuge which is not a conditioned phenomenon.

Ajahn Sumedho, a widely renowned Theravada monk and a disciple of Ajahn Chah, offers a reflection on the Three Refuges that makes each of them immediate and accessible in the moment:

> When we take refuge in the Buddha, it doesn't mean that we take refuge in some historical prophet, but in that which is wise in the universe, in our minds, that which is not separate from us but is more real than anything we can conceive with the mind or experience through the senses. . . . We call it Buddha-wisdom,

other people can call it other things if they want, these are just words. We happen to use the words of our tradition. . . . we're just using the term Buddha-wisdom as a conventional symbol to help remind us to be wise, to be alert, to be awake.[6]

Likewise, when we take refuge in Dhamma we are:

> Not taking refuge in philosophy or intellectual concepts, in theories, in ideas, in doctrines or beliefs of any sort. It is not taking refuge in a belief in Dhamma . . . something we have to find sometime later. The descriptions of the Dhamma keep us in the present, in the here-and-now, unbound by time. Taking refuge is an immediate immanent reflection in the mind . . .

Finally, taking refuge in Sangha, means that

> We take refuge in virtue, in that which is good, virtuous, kind, compassionate and generous . . . We take refuge in that in all of us that intends to do good, which is compassionate and kind and loving towards ourselves and others.

This way of understanding the refuges makes them accessible to all of us, whatever our level of spiritual maturation. It also allows them to be immanent for each of us, whatever insights we might have had. By understanding the refuges as that "in me" which is wise and awake, as the here-and-now, and as goodness, we are using conventions to bring into awareness the aim of the path.

Why Be Moral?

The aim of the Buddha's path is to come to know things as they are, to develop non-attachment, and to undermine self-cherishing. Without the restraint of morality, a person could mindfully tell a lie, take something that belonged to another, or even kill. Typically when we perform these and other wrong actions, our motivation is to satisfy our own desires, aversions, or the illusion of self-cherishing. These, as the Buddha points out, are the three roots of the unwholesome.

51

It might be helpful to look at a few examples. Suppose someone asks you if you read a book, and, though you had not, you say you had read it. One typical motivation for lying is to preserve your image and your desire for others to see you in a certain way. Or suppose you take an apple that belongs to someone else. Why? Typically to satisfy your own desire. Or suppose you kill a deer. Why? Likely for sport, or for a trophy, or to satisfy the desire to eat venison. Or suppose you kill a snake. The motive this time is likely aversion. In each of these cases, one is treating one's own desires as more important than the desire of the other person to hear the truth, the desire of the other person to have an apple, or the desire of the deer or the snake to live. To act in any of these ways reinforces the illusion of a self, self-cherishing, the attitude that "I" am more important than others, as well as desire and attachment. One reason for following the five precepts and Right Livelihood is to avoid reinforcing the unwholesome roots of action that the rest of the practice is encouraging us to abandon.

The Buddha provides a second answer to the "why be moral" question after Ananda asks what "is the object, what is the profit of good conduct?" The Buddha replies:

> Good conduct has freedom from remorse as object and profit; freedom from remorse has joy; joy has rapture; rapture has calm; calm has happiness; happiness has concentration; concentration has seeing things as they really are; seeing things as they really are has revulsion and fading of interest; revulsion and fading of interest have release by knowing and seeing as their object and profit. So you see, Ananda, good conduct leads gradually up to the summit (AN: X, 1).

According to the Buddha, wholesome actions lay the foundation for seeing things as they are.

----

1. Some cite an exchange between the Buddha and Ananda in support of the importance of human friendship and community for those on the path. Ananda says that about half of the holy life consists in righteous friendship, righteous intimacy, and righteous association. The Buddha corrects him, "Not so, Ananda! Very not so, Ananda! Verily the whole of this life in religion consists in righteous friendship, righteous intimacy, righteous association"(S: III, 2, 8). If one reads no further, this passage would support the view that community and friendship play a major role in the holy life according to the Buddha. The passage fails to support this claim. In the next paragraph the Buddha makes clear that he is talking about being "a friend, an intimate, an associate of that which is righteous" and that "the whole of this life in

religion is concerned with friendship, intimacy, association with whatsoever is lovely and righteous"(ibid).

2. Tax resistors who recommend not paying taxes sometimes recommend both not lying on tax forms and giving to a worthy cause an amount of money equal to what the taxes would have been.

3. Ajahn Chah, *Food for the Heart* (Bahn Bung Wai, Thailand: The Sangha, Wat Pah Nonnachat, 1992), p. 59.

4. There are currently no fully ordained nuns in the Theravadin tradition, but the ordination for nuns has been passed on into the Mahayana tradition and some Theravadins hope to bring back full ordination into Theravada Buddhism. Contemporary Theravadin nuns, even though they do not take a full ordination into nuns' *Vinaya*, take upon themselves the ten precepts: the five listed next in the text, and five others that require restraining from (6) eating after noon, (7) dancing, singing, and watching plays or movies for fun; (8) garlands, perfume, and adornment; (9) luxurious beds; (10) accepting or using money.

5. In this paragraph I follow Bhikkhu Bodhi, *Going for Refuge, Taking the Precepts* (Kandy, Sri Lanka: Buddhist Publication Society, 1981), passim.

6. Ajahn Sumedho, "Buddha Dhamma Sangha," in *Now is the Knowing,* op. cit., p. 10. The quote on Dhamma is from p. 14; the quote on Sangha from pp. 16-17.

7

Concentration

The final group of the Eightfold Path includes Right Effort, Right Mindfulness, and Right Concentration. Here the path laid out by the Buddha deviates even further from the conception of philosophy in the West and from the practice of orthodox, nonmystical Western religion.

Right Effort

The Buddha emphasized Right Effort because, from his perspective, realization and insight depend on what we bring to the practice.

> And what, monks, is Right Effort? Here, monks, a monk rouses his will, makes an effort, stirs up energy, exerts his mind and strives to prevent the arising of unarisen evil unwholesome mental states. . . and strives to overcome evil unwholesome mental states that have arisen. He rouses his will . . . and strives to produce unarisen wholesome mental states. He rouses his . . .and strives to maintain wholesome mental states that have arisen, not to let them fade away, to bring them to greater growth, to the full perfection of development. This is called Right Effort. (D: 22, 21)

The Buddha emphasized throughout his life that insight requires effort and his last words were that each of us must strive tirelessly (D: 16, 6.7).

Because we are in a culture that emphasizes competition and teeth-clenching effort, we need to find the balance between too much effort and too little. The Buddha points to this balance in a discussion with a discouraged young monk who, as a layman, had been skillful at playing the lute. The Buddha reminds this monk that when the strings of the lute were too tight he could not play it, nor could he play it when the strings were too slack. He then asks the monk if the lute was fit for playing "when the strings of your lute were neither too taut nor too slack, but were keyed to an even pitch?" When the monk says that the properly tuned lute was fit for playing, the Buddha tells him that his own effort must also be properly tuned, for when effort is too strenuous it leads to restlessness, and when it is too slack it leads to laziness. Therefore, the Buddha concludes, he should practice with a uniform evenness of effort (Vin: i, 181-182).

Right Mindfulness

Right Mindfulness requires being fully aware of what is happening in the moment, as it is, without the complexities added by fear, aversion, desire, longing, or conventional and cultural evaluations.

> And what, monks, is Right Mindfulness? Here, monks, a monk abides contemplating body as body, ardent, clearly aware and mindful, having put aside hankering and fretting for the world; he abides contemplating feelings as feelings . . . .; he abides contemplating mind as mind . . . ; he abides contemplating mind-objects as mind-objects, ardent, clearly aware and mindful, having put aside hankering and fretting for the world. This is called Right Mindfulness (D: 22, 21).

The contemplation of the body as body, of feelings as feelings, of mind as mind, and of mind-objects as mind-objects are the four foundations of mindfulness (M: 10, 2). The Buddha emphasizes mindfulness of breathing as a way to develop these four foundations:

> On whatever occasion a bhikkhu, breathing in long, understands: "I breathe in long," or breathing out long, understands "I breathe out long". . . breathing in short . . .breathing out short . . . breathing in experiencing the whole body . . . breathing out experiencing the whole body ... breathing in tranquillising the bodily formation. . .

breathing out tranquillising the bodily formation . . . on that occasion a bhikkhu abides contemplating the body as a body . . . .

On whatever occasion . . . "I shall breathe in experiencing rapture" . . . breathe out experiencing rapture . . . pleasure . . . the mental formation . . . tranquillising mental formation . . . a bhikkhu abides contemplating feelings as feelings. . . .

On whatever occasion a bhikkhu trains this: "I shall breathe in experiencing the mind" ... breathe out experiencing the mind . . . gladdening the mind . . . concentrating the mind . . . liberating the mind . . . a bhikkhu abides contemplating mind as mind. . . .

On whatever occasion a bhikkhu trains thus: "I shall breathe in contemplating impermanence". . . fading away ... cessation ... relinquishment . . . a bhikkhu abides contemplating mind-objects as mind-objects . . . (M: 118, 23-27).

The Buddha concludes that this "is how mindfulness of breathing, developed and cultivated, fulfils the four foundations of mindfulness" (M: 118, 28).

To be fully mindful is often seen as the pinnacle of Buddhist practice and is an essential step toward liberation. One widely taught technique of developing mindfulness begins with an awareness of how the breath feels throughout the body, then focuses either on how the breath feels as it enters and leaves the nostrils, or on the rise and fall of the abdomen. As one begins to explore how the breath "feels" in the nostrils, one typically finds the in-breath to be cool, the out-breath to be warm, and, accompanying either in-breath or out-breath, there may be pressure, movement, smoothness, sharpness, tickling, or other physical sensations. By focusing on these basic, unexciting sensations one can begin to focus on what is happening in the present moment underneath concepts, expectations, and beliefs.

A concentrated awareness of how the breath feels is an illustration of how one begins to become aware of bodily and mental phenomena that arise in awareness. For example, imagine a pain in the knee: one can focus on this pain, exploring what is there beneath the aversion and the automatic identification of the feeling as painful. What are the sensations under what we label 'pain'? One might find warmth, movement, tingling, pressure, tightness, sharpness. One can then explore what each of these is like. For example, what is this that I am inclined to name 'pressure'? What is this like, underneath any labels? Likewise, one might explore emotions. Where is the anger in the body? What does it feel like? What are its dimensions? Does it move? In these ways one may become aware of what we often barely feel at all, coming to be able to be open to emotions without either repressing them or acting on them but, instead, attending to what they are in the moment.

Metta is a useful tool for exploring inner phenomena, especially those which we take to be negative: dissatisfaction, disappointment, grief, anger, ill-will, loneliness, feelings of insecurity, feelings of anxiety, and all the rest. Metta encourages us to be open and patient with all phenomena without any repulsion or aversion, and helps create a sphere in which we allow inner phenomena to arise and cease for the purpose of investigation. With metta we are better able to notice how these phenomena are, without thinking of them as "my" or "mine." For example, rather than focusing on "my pang of disappointment," one is aware of "pang, here, now." In this way one can cultivate an awareness of how phenomena arise and cease, without complicating our awareness with attachments and aversions.

The practice of being mindful of phenomena as they occur in each moment is a change in the way we generally attend to the external world and to inner phenomena. Typically we aim at goals and are oblivious of what happens along the way. For example, when we eat breakfast many of us are thinking about what we will do later. Those on a morning commute often do not notice the shape of the clouds, or the sunlight filtering through a tree, or the bird sitting on a bush. Many commuters cannot recall any internal or external phenomena during an hour of commuting if nothing out of the ordinary happened. The practice of mindfulness encourages us to develop a habit of mind that involves an awareness of what is happening in the moment, not only when we formally practice, but throughout our lives. In contrast to the commuter who is oblivious of what happens during the commute, the commuter who is practiced in mindfulness will more likely be aware of her bodily sensations, aware of her inner reactions to other commuters, aware of the color of the sky, and aware of the clouds.

The following story illustrates the subtlety of being in the moment. A young monk had just bathed and was drying himself, clad only in a single cloth, when an attractive female deva came and said to him:

> Thou art young, bhikkhu, to have left the world, and callow, black-haired and blessed with the luck of youth; thou hast not in thine early prime had the fun that belongs to natural desires. Take thy fill, bhikkhu, of human pleasures. Give not up the things of the present to pursue that which involves time (S: I, 2, 10).

On the face of it, were the young monk to succumb to the seductive deva we might think that he would be living in the moment. We can, however, distinguish living *in* the moment from living *for* the moment. Living *in* the moment involves mindfulness of how things are in whatever moment and situation we find ourselves. Living *for* the moment involves a pursuit of pleasure and excitement that typically takes our attention away from what is going on in the moment and replaces it with some aim or goal which, if it is attained and is pleasant enough, may momentarily capture our attention.

The young bhikkhu makes this distinction, albeit in different words, in his response to the seductive deva:

> I, friend, have not given up the things of the present to pursue that which involves time. Nay, I have given up that which involves time to pursue the things of the present. Things involving time... are the pleasures of sense, full of suffering, full of anxiety; that way lies abundant disaster. A thing of the present is the Dhamma, not involving time, inviting one to come and see, leading onward, to be regarded by the wise as a personal experience (S: I, 2, 10).

This example, as well as the example of the typical commuter, allow us to answer the concern that Buddhism deadens the practitioner to sensory experience. Our usual habit of mind pushes away the unpleasant, overlooks the ordinary, and aims at the pleasant and exciting, effectively screening out of our awareness of much of what occurs moment by moment. In contrast, it is plausible to think that the practice of mindfulness heightens our awareness of both outer and inner phenomena in every moment of our lives.

Right Concentration

Concentration is unification of the mind (M: I. 301) and, without a unified mind, insight and wisdom are impossible (Dhp. 372). The Buddha tells his disciples that the two factors of concentration and insight are "yoked evenly together" (M: 149, 10). The Buddha states that a person who is concentrated comes to know the impermanence of body, feelings, perception, mental activities, and sense consciousness. The result of these insights is the complete liberation from suffering (S: XXII, 5).

In the texts, the concentration component of the Eightfold Path usually includes the Buddha's description of four meditative states referred to as jhanas:

And what, monks, is Right Concentration? Here, a monk, detached from sense-desires, detached from unwholesome mental states, enters and remains in the first jhana . . . . the second jhana . . . . the third jhana . . . . the fourth jhana . . . (D: 22, 21).

The first jhana "is accompanied by initial and sustained application of mind and filled with rapture and happiness born of seclusion."[1] The phrase "initial application of mind" is the directing of attention to the object of meditation, while the phrase "sustained application of mind" is the continued focus on this object. With continued practice, the mediator enters the second jhana, not needing the factors of initial and sustained application that come to be seen as somewhat coarse compared with the other elements. The second jhana "is free from initial and sustained application but is filled with rapture and happiness born of concentration" (D: 22, 21).

The mind becomes more tranquil and unified in the second jhana and now rapture, which tends towards excitement, seems less refined and is allowed to fade:

> With the fading out of rapture, he dwells in equanimity, mindful and clearly comprehending; and he experiences in his own person that bliss of which the noble ones say: "Happily lives he who is equanimous and mindful"--thus he enters and dwells in the third jhana (D: 22, 21).

When the mediator comes to see happiness as less refined than equanimity, he moves beyond happiness into the fourth jhana "which has neither-pleasure-nor-pain" but has " purity of mindfulness due to equanimity" (D: 22, 21).

Because the four jhanas are part of Right Concentration and so are mentioned at the end of the Eightfold Path, these meditative states may appear to be the culmination of the entire Eightfold Path. It is important to realize that the jhanas, albeit highly concentrated mental states that help counteract the hinderances, are not the aim of the practice. The aim of the practice is the understanding and insight that solve the problem of suffering.

----

1. Bhikkhu Bodhi, *The Noble Eightfold Path* (Buddhist Publication Society: Kandy, Sri Lanka: 1994), p 99. My discussion of the four jhanas is based on Bhikkhu Bodhi, ibid., pp. 95-102. I have also used the translation of the jhanas which Bhikkhu Bodhi provides on p. 99.

8

The Possibility of
Liberation

In this chapter we shall focus on three objections often raised to question whether Buddhism offers a conceptually coherent approach to life. The first of these problems is whether the desire for desirelessness demonstrates the impossibility of abandoning all attachments or desires.[1] The second is that, even if we can show that it is logically possible to be without desires, it is plausible that a person who was attained this state would need a desire to remain that way. The third is whether we can make sense of a coherent pattern of human activity for a person free from desire. If any of these problems is insoluble, then the Buddhist programme, whatever insights it may offer into human life, would ultimately not be coherent.

The Desire for Desirelessness

If a person who wanted to stop suffering tried to move toward becoming desireless, that person would naturally desire to become desireless. If that person now desired to remove this new desire, the desire to do so would be an additional desire, and, apparently, to remove the new desire would require another desire and so on ad infinitum. If this criticism of Theravada

Buddhism were accurate, then there would always be at least one desire remaining for the person trying to remove all desires, and the aim of the Buddhist programme could never be achieved. It would follow that the Buddhist programme, at least as I have characterized it, would be as logically impossible as trying to square a circle.

A practitioner might offer several answers to solve the problem of the desire for desirelessness. One answer suggests that, instead of desiring to become desireless, the practitioner might instead *intend* to work toward the cessation of craving and desire. The problem with this reply is that someone questioning whether Buddhism is logically coherent might question whether intentions are only desires in disguise.[2] A second answer requires the assumption that the Eightfold Path leads to liberation. If we make this assumption, becoming a skilled practitioner of the components of the path would lead to desirlessness. The logic of this answer is akin to the logic of the following: if penicillin will cure Sally's pneumonia, then if Sally takes the penicillin her pneumonia will be cured. Someone examining the merits of Buddhism and questioning the possibility of desirelessness would be reluctant to accept this reply because, by assuming the efficacy of the path, it begs the question and simply assumes that a person can become desireless. The Venerable Ananda, the Buddha's chief disciple, offered a variation of this reply to a questioner:

> That monk who is Arahant, one in whom the asavas [roots of suffering] are destroyed, who has lived the life, done the task, lifted the burden, who is a winner of his own welfare, who has outworn the fetters of rebirth, one who is released by perfect insight,--that desire which he had previously to attain Arahantship, now that Arahantship is won, that appropriate desire is abated (S: v, 273).

Venerable Ananda is making the important point that the desire to seek liberation is appropriate for anyone who would move towards liberation. But the person questioning the possibility of desirelessness would not be satisfied with Ananda's answer to her query since, by assuming the possibility of Arahantship, it assumes precisely what is in question. Since the thought that Buddhism might rest on a logical inconsistency has the potential for blocking a person from investigating it further, we have a strong practical reason for resolving the problem in its own analytical terms.

There is an analytical solution to this problem that does not beg the question. What we are asking is whether there is any state that a person can desire which, if attained, would result in the person's being desireless. One answer to this question is that a person could desire to rid herself of all desires except the desire to do so. Once all other desires were extinguished, the desire to be rid of them would be satisfied, and hence it too would be extinguished.[3] There is also a more common-sense variant of this analytical answer. When we think of the desires that typically cause us suffering--the desire for comfort, for the well-being of others, for affection, for health, for reputation, for money--it makes sense to think that if we did not have these desires, then we would no longer suffer the corresponding frustrations and dissatisfactions. If all such desires were removed, then the person in question would no longer desire to be rid of them and, hence, would be without any desires. From an analytical point of view we seem to have shown that reaching a momentary state in which there are no desires is possible.

The Desire To Remain Desireless

We have assumed, in discussing the problem generated by the desire for desirelessness puzzle, that when a desire is satisfied, it is gone. This is true for what are referred to as "felt" or occurrent desires: if I have a desire for a particular orange, and am given that orange, then I no longer have that desire. A "felt" or occurrent desire involves a favorable regarding or viewing of an object, and often involves an inner tug, or warm feeling, or empty feeling, or tingle, or some other inner sensation (hence the name "felt").[4] Not all desires, however, are occurrent or "felt." Smith, for example, may want more money, even though Smith has no tugs or tingles at this moment about the prospect of having more money because Smith is totally involved in watching the first robin of spring. But Smith does want more money, and under the proper conditions this want will become occurrent. Such background or "waiting" wants are referred to as dispositional desires. The more basic of the two kinds of desires is the occurrent desire, since a dispositional want is only a disposition or propensity to have an occurrent want under certain conditions.

The desire to reach a goal which, when reached, leaves one desireless, is a desire to be a certain kind of person. Such desires are typically dispositional. For example, if I desire to be a good tennis player, and become one, is my desire to be a good tennis player extinguished--or only temporarily satisfied? What happens if, the following season, I slip into mediocrity? We might say that the original desire was extinguished and that I may or may not now have a new desire to become a good tennis player

62

again, or, if I do find myself desiring to be a good tennis player, we might say that the original desire was a dispositional desire and was always "in the background." In the case of Buddhism, however, the desire to be free of all other desires is not only a desire to become a certain kind of person, but also a desire to remain a certain kind of person without backsliding. The only way such a desire can be satisfied is if one never backslides. If one does backslide, the desire to be that kind of person would no longer be satisfied and, one might hope, backsliding would again motivate the person to regain her lost freedom from desire. This suggests that the desire to extinguish all other desires is not only occurrent but is also dispositional, and that the person who has extinguished all occurrent desires would still have a dispositional or background desire to remain free of any occurrent desire.

It follows from this that although we have shown the logical possibility of the cessation of all occurrent desires, we have not yet established the plausibility of the cessation of all dispositional desires. To make plausible the cessation of all desires, occurrent and dispositional, requires that we investigate a fundamental factor that leads to suffering: ignorance.

Ignorance Conditions Desire

As we have seen, the Buddha taught that knowledge *as direct insight* is essential to solve the problem of suffering. One chief insight a person gains in overcoming the ignorance that leads to desire is the insight into the impermanence of all phenomena. Partly as a result of the impermanence of everything, desire leads to suffering, for if we desire and gain anything ordinarily taken to be "permanent"--health, home, reputation, family, the well-being of friends--our desire typically involves the desire to keep what we have. Because everything is changing and passing away, the desire to keep anything will eventually be frustrated. A realization of this fundamental impermanence is central to liberation. The following example illustrates and makes plausible how the awareness of impermanence can undermine the desire for something to remain as it is.

Suppose Sara, an adult, has lived her entire life next to a northern California beach and has daily experienced the tides, which rise and fall an average of over five feet where she lives. Imagine that she takes her eight year old nephew, Richard, who has never even seen the ocean, to the beach. Richard is from the Midwest and the largest body of water he has experienced is Lake Michigan, which has a negligible tide. When they reach the beach, it is low tide. Sara and Richard together build a large and beautiful sandcastle only a few yards from the wash of the waves. After the tide turns and begins coming in, it is obvious to Sara that their sandcastle will soon be completely washed away. Precisely because Sara knows the inevitable force of the rising tide almost as well as she knows anything from experience, we can understand how it would be hard for her to be attached to the longevity of their sandcastle. Richard, however, has a radically different awareness of what is going on. We imagine him wanting the sandcastle to remain standing and that he struggles to protect the sandcastle from the incoming tide by piling up more and more sand around it. Of course it is hopeless. Sara knows this, but Richard suffers as his efforts to protect the sandcastle from destruction begin to fail. Importantly, what distinguishes Sara from Richard is their knowledge: no other factor seems able to account for their markedly differing degrees of desire. Because Sara knows that a sandcastle in the tide zone will be washed away and the debris submerged under the rising tide, she cannot desire the sandcastle to last, or at least not to the same degree as Richard does. Hence, the most plausible account we can give of the difference in the degree of the desires of these two people is their knowledge of the power of tides (in the sense in which knowledge is realization and different from mere information).

This example shows the plausibility of the claim that a realization of the impermanence of entities makes us less able to desire them to be otherwise. We may use this conclusion to illustrate the plausibility of a much larger point. According to the Buddha, everything that we are involved in trying to get, maintain, or protect--health, relationships, job, professional status--has the same essential characteristic of Sara's and Richard's sandcastle: all this is in process of passing away.

> All that is mine, all that is beloved and pleasing to me, will someday be otherwise, will someday be separated from me (AN: iii, 71-72).

Indeed, whatever phenomenon any of us can experience is, like a cloud or a sandcastle, a ceasing thing. Hence, it is plausible that the person who clearly sees this will not be attached to any of it at all.

If the argument above is correct, we have shown the possibility of desirelessness. It is plausible to think that the person who has an awareness of the nature of all phenomena, including their essential impermanence, will not have any occurrent desires again. Since there will not be any more occurrent desires, it makes no sense to claim that there are any underlying dispositional desires, since a dispositional desire is nothing more than a disposition for occurrent desires to arise. Hence, there need be no background dispositional desire--no desire to remain desireless--for a person to remain free from occurrent desire. For such a being, there will be no desires or attachments of any kind at all.

Action Without Desire

This possibility leads to a third concern often raised about Buddhism: the worry that without desire a person would be so indifferent as to be unable to act in any coherent way at all, much less act in the compassionate way exemplified by the Buddha. We begin answering this concern by reflecting on our ordinary actions.

Imagine that you turn your key to the right in an automobile's ignition. You just turn the key: you have no apparent desire to turn it, and no thought of having to turn it, and likely you are thinking about something other than the action of turning the key. Or: imagine you are leisurely walking down a street and you brush against an elderly person who is struggling to keep from dropping some shopping bags. You help quickly without any thought as to whether helping is in your interest, or is something you ought to do. Or again: someone asks you for directions and you know the information requested. Again you just act, giving the directions without any conscious decision or desire to do so.

In each of these examples we can imagine a person acting only after a conscious decision or a "felt" desire to do so, and for each of us there may have been a time when such a mental event was required to turn a key in an ignition, help with bags, or give directions. But now that such ways of acting have become habitual, that's the way we are: we just do such actions. Habitual actions show that coherent human action is possible without a desire to act in the requisite way.[5] Perhaps most of our actions are desireless in this way: the way we sit, hold a pen, walk, eat soup, raise a hand to ask a question, respond to our name being called, and so on.

This response to the concern that action is impossible without desire may seem incomplete. First, habitual actions are rooted in desire--at one point, for example, we desired to learn how to start a car, and our first attempts were filled with the appropriate inner tugs until we mastered the actions involved. In addition, a life of habit does not seem to be a good way to avoid suffering, for when habitual action is blocked, frustration and suffering often result. Finally, actions like starting a car occur within a context of desire, for when a person starts her car, presumably she does so because she wants to go somewhere. I shall focus on the last two concerns in turn, after noting that the first provides no difficulty for the Buddhist. The Buddha does not claim that we begin without desire, only that there is no desire when the process is completed.[6]

In the foregoing I have referred to patterns of coherent human activity that do not require desire as habitual. It is more appropriate to refer to these patterns of activity as skills. Acquiring a habit is troublesome for the Buddhist in two ways that acquiring a skill is not. If Mary is a person who gardens in an habitual way, and always plants tomatoes on the last published frost date for her area, she may well be frustrated when the weather is unseasonably cold and her tomatoes freeze. But if she is a person who gardens in a skillful way, there is nothing about her way of gardening that will lead to frustration in these conditions. A person's gardening skillfully simply requires that the person exemplify good gardening principles as well as possible given a particular soil and a particular microclimate. Insofar as acting skillfully is the whole account of what Mary is doing, then as a gardener she will not be frustrated if in exercising her skills she needs to change her plans in order to accommodate changing weather patterns. As long as she is only trying to garden skillfully and is not attached to the results, she will no more be frustrated when she needs to cover her tomato plants at night for another week than she would be if, while only trying to play skillfully, she lost her most skillful game of chess to a player whom she knew to be much better than herself. Secondly, habits are notoriously blind, as blind as desire, whereas skills require constant awareness and adaptability to changing conditions. The gardener who habitually gardens in a particular fashion may have plants die in an unusually cold spring, whereas the skillful gardener will more likely be aware of the new conditions and more able to take them into consideration.[7] If her plants die, and of course there are conditions in which the world's best gardener cannot prevent plants from dying, it will not be because of a lack of awareness or due to her own attachment to a particular way of gardening.

Although these and other skillful activities may, like habits, account for coherent patterns of human activity unmotivated by desire, these patterns of activities typically occur in contexts in which desires play a fundamental motivational role. For example, a person gardens because she wants vegetables, or flowers, or just to be working with plants. Is it possible to act unmotivated by desire and without a context of desire? Is it possible for an entire life to be devoid of desire?

To answer this question we will first turn to an apparently unrelated question: why does Buddhism point toward compassion in addition to pointing toward desirelessness? One answer to this question begins with the key observation that compassion is a natural antidote to desire.[8] But even compassion may embroil us in desires for the well-being of others. I may begin to identify with the desires of those whom I am trying to help, or I may become frustrated at my own inadequacy. At best, then, compassion may seem only an adequate antidote to egoistical desires. Nonetheless, this move away from egoistical desires is really a move to an entirely new position: the goal of becoming an exemplification of compassion. If we take becoming an exemplification of compassion as a realizable possibility, we can see how coherent human action without desire is possible.

Becoming fully compassionate is part of the path towards liberation from suffering. Once one is fully compassionate, there is never an occasion for frustration over the suffering of others. If one can do something to relieve the suffering of another, and this is the overall compassionate act, one does so. If there is suffering that cannot be relieved, an understanding of this reality would prevent frustration or any other suffering for a fully compassionate person--much as Sara, because she realizes the impossibility of protecting sandcastles in a rising tide, need not suffer because the tide is washing away her sandcastle. In all of this, because being compassionate requires alertness and allaying suffering within ones own being, the compassionate person will care for her mind, heart, and body. Likewise, because being compassionate requires being in relation to others, the compassionate person will nourish noble friendships and her ties to her family and the various communities of which she is a member. In these ways compassion may inform and guide an entire life.

Once the way of compassion is fully exemplified, once one becomes totally and skillfully compassionate, one no longer has any desire to conform to this way of being. This is just one's nature, the way one is, and so these traits are naturally exemplified by one's nature. An exemplar of all of this, a skillfully compassionate being, fully awake and nonattached, is a Buddha.

----

1. Since this and the following problems are articulated in terms of desire, it is important to note that we could also frame them in the language of attachment and non-attachment. Likewise, we could also restate the solutions that follow in terms of attachment and non-attachment. This is important since, if we think of the Buddha as saying that we must *let go* of desire, the focus is initially on the eventual cessation of our *attachment* to desire.

2. I am indebted to Ajahn Sumedho for the relevance of the distinction between intention and desire. There is another distinction that also promises to solve the problem. A Kantian might reply that a person could just "will" to become desireless

and act accordingly. However, the analytical questioner will not accept as noncontroversial that these "willings" fail to express desires. To rest the defense of the rationality of Buddhism on such a controversial claim would not satisfy those who took the problem seriously.

3. This solution is discussed by Wayne Alt, "There is No Paradox of Desire in Buddhism," *Philosophy East and West* Vol. 30, October, 1980, p. 527. Neither Alt nor his critics consider the objection discussed in the text about the problem of dispositional desires.

4. Here I am following Alvin Goldman's account of occurrent and dispositional wants in *A Theory of Human Action* (Englewood Cliffs, N.J.: Prentice-Hall, 1970), pp. 86-99.

5. It may be objected that every action, habitual or otherwise, is motivated by an occurrent desire. The chief problem with this objection is that nothing will count against it. If upon introspection no desires are discovered, then, because the criticism is assumed true, the critic assumes either that a desire was present which was overlooked in introspection or that the desire in question was unconscious. Such criticism assumes an answer to the question we are asking, and in this way simply begs the question. Do I have a desire to turn the ignition key a quarter to the right? I may, but the key point is that I also may not, and that is all the Buddhist needs to defeat the claim that all acts are motivated by desire.

6. See A: ii, 144-147; and S: LI, VII, II, V.

7. Gilbert Ryle makes similar observations about skills. See *The Concept of Mind* (London: Barnes and Noble, 1949), pp. 42 and 45. As Ryle points out, having a skill involves being able to innovate in situations that are new. For example, the skillful driver has never "foreseen the runaway donkey, yet he is not unprepared for it. His readiness to cope with such emergencies would show itself in the operations he would perform, if they were to occur" (op. cit., p. 48).

8. I am indebted to Moreland Perkins for this observation. Note that compassion can also be an antidote for suffering. For example, a person suffering a significant monetary loss may find her pain and underlying desires are diminished when she focuses on the plight of war victims who have lost all their possessions, their families, and their communities.

9

Mahayana Buddhism

We have been exploring the basic teachings of the Buddha and have relied on the Pali texts of Theravada Buddhism as our source of these teachings. Another major form of Buddhism is Mahayana Buddhism. The texts of Mahayana Buddhism are written in Sanskrit, whereas the texts of Theravada are in Pali, so many terms in prior chapters will now appear in Sanskrit. Mahayana Buddhists referred to the form of Buddhism we have been examining as Hinayana Buddhism [small (hina) vehicle (yana) Buddhism] because it emphasized the enlightenment of the individual. In contrast, Mahayanists referred to their form of Buddhism as the great (maha) vehicle (yana) because it emphasized the enlightenment of all sentient beings. Some who practiced what the Mahayanists called Hinayana Buddhism came to call their vehicle Theravada Buddhism, and we will continue to use this name in these final chapters.

Mahayana Buddhism rests on the basic teachings of the Buddha: the Four Noble Truths, the Eightfold Path, and insight into conditioned phenomena as impermanent, not-self, and ultimately unsatisfactory. As we shall see below, Mahayana Buddhism emphasizes selfless compassion and the realization of the lack of any permanent, substantial nature to phenomena. Whether this emphasis marks a difference with Theravada Buddhism or not, Mahayana Buddhism rests on the same basic teachings as Theravada Buddhism and, for this reason, the reader primarily interested in Mahayana or one of its variants has been exploring pertinent material for the past eight chapters. In this chapter we limit ourselves to the exploration of the ways in which the Mahayana tradition seems to differ from the Theravada.

69

The Bodhisattva Ideal

According to the *Lankavatara Sutra*, a central Mahayana sutra (Sanskrit for 'sutta'), practitioners of Mahayana Buddhism eventually achieve perfect understanding of the way things are. Living out the Bodhisattva ideal, these Mahayana practitioners refuse to enter Nirvana (Sanskrit for 'Nibbana') until all sentient beings are enlightened. At this stage they become aware of the part they are to play in carrying out their vow to work tirelessly for the liberation of all beings and they experience a "turning-about" from egoism to universal compassion in their deepest consciousnesses. These practitioners come to experience the Bodhisattva's Nirvana, losing themselves in the bliss of perfect self-yielding.[1]

Shantideva expresses this emphasis on compassion in the following passages from *A Guide to the Bodhisattva's Way of Life:*[2]

> May I be the doctor and the medicine
> And may I be the nurse
> For all sick beings in the world
> Until everyone is healed (Bdh: iii, 8).

> May a rain of Food and drink descend
> To clear away the pain of thirst and hunger,
> And during the aeon of famine
> May I myself change into food and drink (Bdh iii, 9).

> May I become an inexhaustible treasure
> For those who are poor and destitute;
> May I turn into all things they could need
> And may these be placed close beside them (Bdh:iii, 10).

> May all the pains of living creatures
> Ripen (solely) upon myself,
> And through the might of the Bodhisattva Sangha
> May all beings experience happiness (Bdh: x, 56).

Mahayana Buddhism supports this emphasis on compassion with two metaphysical claims. The first is that all sentient creatures share the same fundamental Buddha-nature. As Geshey Ngawang Dhargyey writes, "The

70

Buddha Nature lies within everyone--one must realize this and live accordingly."[3] Since we share the same fundamental nature with other sentient beings, it is not unnatural for us to want to relieve the suffering of fellow beings who are exactly like us in their fundamental nature. The second is that each of us has been reincarnated over and over again for countless aeons. As a result, there is no sentient creature who has not been the mother of each of us in a prior life. Viewing each sentient creature as a mother, it becomes difficult not to take a perspective of universal compassion.

The notion of being happy in the service of others is not one that is widely acknowledged, but Shantideva pointed out what many find to be true in their own experience:

> Whatever joy there is in this world
> All comes from desiring others to be happy,
> And whatever suffering there is in this world
> All comes from desiring myself to be happy (Bdh: viii, 129).

The Mahayana emphasis on compassion leads to practices that are not part of the Theravada tradition, for example, visualization meditations that aim to take upon oneself the suffering of others.

Emptiness

Another major difference between Theravada and Mahayana Buddhism is that Mahayana develops and puts a central emphasis on the idea of emptiness. While recognizing that all phenomena are impermanent, not-self, and ultimately unsatisfactory, Mahayana texts emphasize that all phenomena are also empty (sunya) and their ultimate nature is emptiness or voidness (sunyata). The best known source of this claim is the widely quoted stanza from the *Heart Sutra*:

> Form is emptiness, emptiness is not different from form, neither is form different from emptiness, indeed, emptiness is form.[4]

The *Heart Sutra* is not claiming that things do not exist (nihilism). In fact, the last clause clearly implies that where there is emptiness, there is form. The statement that form is empty typically is understood as saying that no form is a continuing self-subsistent entity.

71

Delightful Conundrums

If all phenomena are empty, then we might conclude that there really are no persons and hence no one whose suffering we need to try to alleviate. Likewise, we plausibly might conclude that there really are no teachings, no teachers, and no one to be taught. These are the puzzling but delightful conundrums we can create by mixing the conventional designation of terms with their ultimate realities. This is made clear in the *Diamond Sutra*. The Buddha asks Subhuti:

> If any disciple were to say that the Tathagata, in his teachings, has constantly referred to himself, other selves, living beings, a Universal Self, what think you, Subhuti? Would that disciple have understood the meaning of what I have been teaching?
> Subhuti replied:--No, Blessed Lord. That disciple would not have understood the meaning of the Lord's teachings. For when the Lord has referred to them he has never referred to their actual existence; he has only used the words as figures and symbols. It is only in that sense that they can be used, for conceptions, and ideas, and limited truths, and Dharmas have no more reality than have matter and phenomena.[5]

The Buddha agrees with Subhuti's answer, stating that practitioners "ought thus to see, to perceive, to know, to understand, and to realize that all things and all Dharmas are no-things, and, therefore, they ought not to conceive within their minds any arbitrary conceptions whatever." As if to emphasize this point, at the end of the *Diamond Sutra* the Buddha asks Subhuti:

> What think you, Subhuti? Has the Tathagata given you any definite teaching in the scripture?
> No, Blessed Lord! The Tathagata has not given any definite teaching in this Scripture.

Subhuti had pointed out, earlier in the sutra, that the Tathagata cannot teach any fixed system because what the Tathagata teaches is ineffable. All of this is part of an overall theme which Subhuti expressed when he said that beings are "not enlightened by fixed teachings but by an intuitive process that is spontaneous and natural."[6]

Mahayana and Theravada Compared

Mahayana Buddhism's teachings on a shared Buddha-nature, on sunyata, and on the Bodhisattva ideal, seem initially different from what we see in the Pali texts of Theravada Buddhism. How different are these elements from what we find in that source of the Buddha's basic teachings?

As we have seen, when the Buddha was asked metaphysical questions that could lead to a response pointing to shared Buddha-nature, the Buddha always refused to answer such questions. On the other hand, the Buddha did point to the unconditioned. And there is awareness. To say more would be to misrepresent the Pali texts, but it is not clear that the idea of a shared Buddha-nature is inconsistent with the insights to which the Buddha pointed.

The idea of emptiness or voidness, which is also found but not developed or emphasized in the Theravada texts,[7] is often used to indicate a middle way between annihilationism and eternalism. Nagarjuna, the great philosopher of Mahayana, argued for an interpretation of sunyata that brings this aspect of Mahayana in line with the historical teachings of the Buddha that point to a Middle way.[8] Regardless of the outcome of Nagarjuna's analysis, it is plausible that the word 'sunyata' points to what is already a central insight in the Theravada tradition.

The shift from the Theravadin ideal of the Arhant (Sanskrit for the Pali 'Arahant') to the Mahayana ideal of the Bodhisattva, and the corresponding emphasis on compassion, does seem to be a significant shift from what we find in the Theravada texts. While in Theravada Buddhism there is an important role to be played by compassion, the role played by compassion in Mahayana is more than important, it is stage center. Does this difference make a difference?

It may. For example, consider vegetarianism. The classical locus within Mahayana Buddhism on this issue is Chapter Eight of the *Lankavatara Sutra*. In this sutra Mahamati, a Bodhisattva-Mahasattva, asks the Buddha about "the merit and vice of meat-eating."[9] The Buddha responds that "the Bodhisattva, whose nature is compassion, is not to eat any meat." The Buddha provides numerous reasons for not eating meat, and at one point asks rhetorically:

> How can the Bodhisattva-Mahasattva who desires to approach all living beings as if they were himself and to practice the Buddha-truths, eat the flesh of any living being that is of the same nature as himself?

73

If a person continually reminds herself that all sentient beings have Buddha-nature or are to her like a mother, it is plausible that this might not only influence her choices about what to eat, but all her choices.

Compassion also plays a central role in the lives of Tibetan Buddhists, who follow the Mahayana tradition but typically are not vegetarian. The Chinese invaded Tibet in 1950 and since then they have destroyed most of the monasteries and killed thousands of monks and nuns as well as hundreds of thousands of Tibetans. The Chinese have also colonized Tibet with ethnic Chinese who now outnumber ethnic Tibetans. And yet, in the face of this, Tibetan monks and nuns still emphasize compassion. Consider, for example, the story of one monk who was in a Chinese prison for twenty years and experienced terrible brutality as well as witnessed the torture and death of many Tibetans. This monk, Palden Gyatso, told his Holiness the Dalai Lama that he, Palden Gyatso, had truly been in danger. When the Dalai Lama asked him what the danger was, Palden Gyatso told the Dalai Lama that he was in danger of giving into anger. Or consider the story of a Tibetan nun who has been imprisoned and tortured and witnessed the torture, rape and murder of other nuns in prison. When she was asked what she did with the rage she must have felt towards her own torturer, she said: "No... it's much larger than that. If he [the torturer] didn't do it, he probably couldn't feed his family. He doesn't know what he's doing. I pray for his future lives."[10] Out of compassion she renounced anger in the face of incredible brutality.

These reflections and examples suggest that the shift from the ideal of the Arhant to the Bodhisattva ideal does lead to practical differences. Yet even this may not fully resolve the issue. Two friends became Theravada Buddhist monks. One, Nyanaponika Thera, remained a Theravada monk while the other became a Tibetan lama known in the West as Lama Anagarika Govinda. Toward the end of his life a visitor asked Nyanaponika Thera about the differences between his path and that of Lama Anagarika Govinda. Nyanaponika Thera replied: "My friend cited the Bodhisattva Vow as the reason for his switch to Mahayana, but I could not see the force of his argument. For if one were to transcend self-centeredness completely, as the Arahat seeks to do, what would be left but compassion?"[11]

---

1. *The Lankavatara Sutra*, trans. by Daisetz Teitaro Suzuki (Routledge and Kegan Paul Ltd.; London, 1973), Chapter Eleven. There is a widely accessible translation of this sutra in *The Buddhist Bible*, ed. Dwight Goddard (Boston: Beacon Press, 1970).

2. Acharya Shantideva, *A Guide to the Bodhisattva's Way of Life*, translated by Stephen Batchelor (Dharamsala: Library of Tibetan Works and Archives, 1979). In what follows I refer to this work as 'Bdh'.

3. Geshey Ngawang Dhargyey, *Tibetan Tradition of Mental Development* (Dharamsala: Library of Tibetan Works and Archives, 1974), p. 86.

4. *A Buddhist Bible*, op. cit., p. 85.

5. *A Buddhist Bible*, ibid., p. 101.

6. *A Buddhist Bible*, ibid., p. 102.

7. At M: 43.33 we find: "And what, friend, is the deliverance of mind through voidness? Here a bhikkhu . . .reflects thus: 'This is void of a self or of what belongs to a self.'" The *Majjhima Nikaya Atthakatha* claims this deliverance is insight into the voidness of self in persons and things. The notion of voidness is also found in M: 121 and M: 122.

8. See David J. Kalupahana, *Nagarjuna: The Philosophy of the Middle Way* (Albany: State University of New York Pres, 1986), pp. 83-90, 307-308, 339-341, and passim.

9.*The Lankavatara Sutra*, trans. by Daisetz Teitaro Suzuki, op.cit., Chapter Eight, p. 212.

10. Richard Gere, "Pilgrimage," *Shambhala Sun* (May, 1999), p. 35.

11. Cited and quoted in Huston Smith, *The World's Religions* (San Francisco: Harper, 1991), p. 127.

10

Zen Buddhism

The first form of Mahayana Buddhism to develop a presence in America was Zen (Japanese for Ch'an) Buddhism.[1] The history of Zen Buddhism begins with Bodhidharma, who in the fifth century traveled from India to China where he introduced Mahayana Buddhism. Bodhidharma taught the *Lankavatara Sutra* and by legend established "wall gazing" as a method of "just sitting" meditation.

Zen was introduced to Japan in the seventh and eighth centuries, though it did not flourish until Eisai established the Rinzai school at the end of the twelfth century. In the next century Dogen established the Soto school. Dogen taught zazen ("sitting meditation"), the point of which is not to focus the mind on anything, but to free the mind from any attachment. Rinzai and Soto today are the two dominant traditions of Zen Buddhism in Japan.

A striking method used by Zen masters, and often associated with the Rinzai school, is the koan. A koan is a verbal riddle or problem that eludes any straightforward rational answer and seems designed to cause the practitioner to break through the encumbered rational mind so that a flash of insight (satori) can occur. A practitioner working with a koan will have regular meetings with her teacher, though these meetings may only last for a few minutes, since a skilled teacher will quickly notice whether the student has experienced the requisite breakthrough. One of the best known koans is: "What is the sound of one hand clapping?"

Although Zen is a form of Mahayana Buddhism and rests on the same teachings, there are differences that stem from the influence of Taoism. Sengstan, the third Zen patriarch, expresses some of these in the following:

> The Great Way is not difficult
> for those who have no preferences. . . .
> If you wish to see the truth
> then hold no opinions for or against anything.
> To set up what you like against what you dislike
> is the disease of the mind....
>
> To deny the reality of things
> is to miss their reality;
> to assert the emptiness of things
> is to miss their reality.
> The more you talk and think about it,
> the further astray you wander from the truth.
> Stop talking and thinking
> and there is nothing you will not be able to know. . . .
>
> Words! The Way is beyond language,
> for in it there is no yesterday, no tomorrow, no today.[2]

As this passage from the third patriarch reveals, Zen abandons the thinking and argumentation we find in some Mahayana texts and describes as mental disease any opinions "for and against." The danger of holding views and opinions, which the Buddha clearly warned against, is that they can block us from insight and understanding, as Nan-in tried to teach a professor:

> Nan-in, a Japanese master during the Meiji era (1868-1912), received a university professor who came to inquire about Zen. Nan-in served tea. He poured his visitor's cup full, and then kept on pouring. The professor watched the overflow until he could no longer restrain himself. "It is overfull. No more will go in!"
> "Like this cup," Nan-in said, "you are full of your own opinions and speculations. How can I show you Zen unless you first empty your cup?"[3]

The following four lines, summing up the message of Bodhidharma, characterize Zen as it developed in China:

A special tranmission outside the scriptures;
No dependence upon words and letters;
Direct pointing at the soul of man;
Seeing into one's nature and the attainment of Buddhahood.[4]

Although much in Zen illustrates these lines, the following Zen story clearly illustrates the importance of direct transmission without a reliance on texts.

Zen master Mu-nan had only one student, Shoju. Mu-nan called Shoju into his room and told him that he, Shoju, was the only one who could pass on the teachings. Mu-nan offered Shoju a book.

> "Here is a book. It has been passed down from master to master for seven generations. I also have added many points according to my understanding. The book is very valuable, and I am giving it to you to represent your successorship."
> "If the book is such an important thing, you had better keep it," Shoju replied. "I received your Zen without writing and am satisfied with it as it is."
> "I know that," said Mu-nan. "Even so, this work has been carried from master to master for seven generations, so you may keep it as a symbol of having received the teachings. Here."
> The two happened to be talking before a brazier. The instant Shoju felt the book in his hands he thrust it into the flaming coals. He had no lust for possessions.
> Mu-nan, who never had been angry before, yelled: "What are you doing!"
> Shoju shouted back: "What are you saying!"[5]

This story characterizes the radical shift Zen makes from other forms of Buddhism.[6] One can not easily imagine a Theravada monk or a Tibetan monk throwing a text handed down for generations into a fire. Yet this story is also a clue as to how Zen transmits the Buddha's insights. When a teaching points to a reality, the danger always is that one takes knowing the teaching for knowing the reality. A key dynamic of Zen is to overcome this error and transmit awakening with precision. According to D. T. Suzuki,

> The claim of the Zen followers that they are transmitting the essence of Buddhism is based on their belief that Zen takes hold of the enlivening spirit of the Buddha, stripped of all its historical and doctrinal garments.[7]

78

In practice, according to Suzuki, Zen abandoned the style of Indian Buddhism in order to transmit the essential insights more directly.

One might wonder whether Zen has given up more than just style. The Zen masters do not think so. Consider the comments of Ho-yen (Fa-yen) of Gosozan (Wu-tsu-shan) on the question of whether there is any difference between the teachings of the Zen Patriarch and the teachings in the Sutras. "When water is scooped in the hands," said Ho-yen Gosozan, "the moon is reflected in them; when the flowers are handled, the scent soaks into the robe."[8]

It would be easy to be misled by the poetic expression of the Zen masters into thinking that Zen does not require the most strenuous effort. The following story about Suiwo clarifies any misunderstanding on this point. A student had come to Suiwo from a southern island of Japan.

> Suiwo gave him the problem, "Hear the sound of one hand."
> The pupil remained three years but could not pass this text. One night he came in tears to Suiwo. "I must return south in shame and embarrassment," he said, "for I cannot solve my problem."
> "Wait one week more and meditate constantly," advised Suiwo. Still no enlightenment came to the pupil. "Try for another week," said Suiwo. The pupil obeyed, but in vain.
> "Still another week." Yet this was of no avail. In despair the student begged to be released, but Suiwo requested another meditation of five days. They were without result. Then he said: "Meditate for three days longer, then if you fail to attain enlightenment, you had better kill yourself."
> On the second day the pupil was enlightened.[9]

Zen often seems to lead to insight only after an intense effort and suffering that forces one back on oneself. "Zen is an experience actual and personal, and not knowledge to be gained by analysis or comparison," according to Suzuki.[10] And of course this requires effort and focus. "If you want to seek the Buddha, you ought to see into your own Nature," Suzuki writes. "If, instead of seeing into your own Nature, you turn away and seek the Buddha in external things, you will never get at him."[11]

All of this seems difficult and, yet, when we read the words of other Zen masters, it still seems easy. When Bankei says that his miracle is that "when I am hungry, I eat; when I am tired, I sleep," isn't this what we already do? The Zen master does not thinks so. Most of us are never wholly mindful of what we are doing: when eating, we are often absent-mindedly preoccupied with something in the future or the past; when going to bed, we may be planning what we will do the next morning or lost in fantasy.[12] Our everyday habit of mind to hold tight to our opinions, to attach to desires, and to be judgemental keep us from being fully in the moment. Consider the revealing story of two monks, Tanzen and Ekido:

> Tanzan and Ekido were once traveling together down a muddy road. A heavy rain was still falling. Coming around a bend, they met a lovely girl in a silk kimono and sash, unable to cross the intersection. "Come on, girl," said Tanzan at once. Lifting her in his arms, he carried her over the mud.
> Ekido did not speak again until that night when they reached a lodging temple. Then he could no longer restrain himself. "We monks don't go near females," he told Tanzan, "especially not young and lovely ones. It is dangerous. Why did you do that?"
> "I left the girl there," said Tanzan. "Are you still carrying her?"[13]

Zen contronts head-on the difficulty that, however one points to the moment or to realization, the target is always beyond language.

> The monk asks the Master, "How may I enter the Way?", and the Master, pointing to the mountain spring, responds, "Do you hear the sound of that torrent? There you may enter." Another time Master and monk are walking upon the mountain, and the Master asks, "Do you smell the mountain laurel?" "Yes." "There, I have held nothing back from you."[14]

Subtle, beautiful, and always pointing, sometimes so clearly that becoming attached to the finger that does the pointing is almost impossible:

> Kakua visited China and accepted the true teaching. He did not travel while he was there. Meditating constantly, he lived on a remote part of a mountain. Whenever people found him and asked him to preach he would say a few words and then move to another part of the mountain where he could be found less easily. The emperor heard about Kakua when he returned to Japan and asked him to preach Zen for his edification and that of his subjects. Kakua stood before the emperor in silence. He then produced a flute from the folds of his robe, and blew one short note. Bowing politely, he disappeared.[15]

----

1. At the Chicago World's Fair in 1893, a Rinzai Zen master was one of the representatives of Buddhism at the World Parliament of Religions. The Zen master returned in 1905 for a visit, and subsequently three of his closest disciples came to the America. Two founded Zen groups and the third was D.T. Suzuki who influenced the understanding of Zen through his writings. See Richard H. Robinson and Willard L. Johnson, *The Buddhist Religion: A Historical Introduction* (Belmont, CA: Wadsworth Publishing Co., 1982), pp. 216-217.

2. *Hsin Hsin Ming* (New York: Zen Center, 1979). Compare Lao Tzu:
"Existence is beyond the power of words to define...
The universe, like a bellows, is always emptying, always full:
Men come to their wit's end arguing about it
And had better meet it as the marrow."
Lao Tzu, in the *Tao Te Ching*, translated as *The Way of Life*, Witter Bynner (New York: Capricorn Books, 1962), pp. 25 and 28.

3. "A Cup of Tea," *Zen Flesh, Zen Bones*, compiled by Paul Reps (New York: Doubleday, 1957): p. 5 .

4. D.T. Suzuki, *Zen Buddhism*, ed. by William Barrett (Garden City, New York: Doubleday and Company, 1956), p. 61.

5. "What Are You Doing! What Are You Saying!", Reps, op. cit., pp. 59-60.

6. Physical labor is another integral (and required) element in Zen training and involves hoeing fields, picking tea leaves, cooking, washing dishes, chopping wood, and carrying water--each practiced as a meditation of moment-by-moment mindfulness. See Richard H. Robinson and Willard L. Johnson, op. cit., pp. 181-182.

7. Suzuki, op. cit., p. 41.

8. Ibid., p. 58.

9. "Three Days More," Reps, op. cit., p. 28.

10. Suzuki, op. cit., p. 20.

11. Ibid., p. 88.

12. Based on William Barrett, in Suzuki, op. cit., p. xvi.

13. "Muddy Road, " Reps, op. cit., p. 18.

14. William Barrett, in Suzuki, op. cit., p. xv.

15. "One Note of Zen," Reps, op. cit., p. 60.

11

Tibetan Buddhism and Vajrayana

The most widely known and respected Buddhist in the world is His Holiness the Dalai Lama. Winner of the Nobel Peace prize in 1989, His Holiness is a practitioner of Vajrayana. Vajrayana, the Diamond (vajra) vehicle (yana), results from the transmission of Mahayana and Tantric practices from India into Tibet.

Shortly after the teachings of Buddhism first reached Tibet in the sixth century, Tibetans invented a written version of their language. This would prove crucial not only for the development of Vajrayana, but also for the preservation of Indian Sanskrit Buddhist texts, since in the following centuries many of the Sanskrit Buddhist texts in India were either lost or destroyed by the ravages of time.

By the middle of the eighth century, Tibetans were translating Buddhist texts from both Indian and Chinese sources. The Indian Mahayana scholar and philosopher Shantarakshita was invited to Tibet and, at his encouragement, Padma Sambhava also came. Together they co-founded the first monastic complex at Samye. Padma Sambhava is acknowledged as the founder of the Nyingma tradition of Vajrayana.

A century later, with the Indian and Chinese Buddhist traditions in Tibet in conflict, the Tibetan king arranged a debate for adjudicating the dispute. At issue was the Chinese view that enlightenment was "sudden," and so did not require arduous practice, and the Indian view that a "gradual path" was necessary. Many sources claim that the Indian Mahayanists won the debate, and this view of history is supported by the subsequent decline of Ch'an Buddhism in Tibet. Subsequently Tibetans published a Sanskrit-Tibetan glossary of Buddhist terms and continued the translation of Indian Sanskrit Buddhist texts.

After more than a hundred years of persecution of Buddhism in Tibet, the Bengali Buddhist scholar Atisha was persuaded to come to Tibet. Atisha spent seventeen years in Tibet, where he transmitted the teachings to the layman Dromtonpa. The Kadam tradition of Tibetan arose from these teachings. Later Marpa, a disciple of Naropa and the teacher of the great yogi hermit Milarepa, founded the Kargu tradition. In the fourteenth century Tsongkapa founded the Gelugpa tradition, to which His Holiness the Dalai Lama belongs. During this period of activity, Tibetans studied under Indian masters both in Nepal and Northern India.

Tibet, being isolated and protected by the Himalayas, emphasized the practice of spirituality as perhaps no country ever has. One out of every five persons was a monk or a nun. Tibetans developed, practiced, and refined techniques of meditation for many hundreds of years without outside disturbance until the Chinese invasion in the twentieth century. The practice of spirituality was the main "industry" of Tibet and, because the Chinese invasion forced many thousands of monks, tulkus (reincarnates) and lamas (masters) out of Tibet, Vajrayana has been the great "export" from Tibet to the rest of the world.

The emphasis in Vajrayana, like the emphasis in Mahayana, is on the realization of sunyata and the practice of the Bodhisattva way of life. Within Tibetan Buddhism there are two classifications of practices and teachings. One is based on the sutras and is sometimes referred to as sutrayana. The second are the secret teachings of trantrayana that require a guru who can give an initiation.

The sutrayana path plays a central role in Tibetan Buddhism and is an expression of what we have already examined in the chapter on Mahayana Buddhism. The sutrayana path emphasizes renunciation, and the path develops from the basic teachings of the Buddha expressed in Theravada Buddhism.[1] Great emphasis is placed on rebirth in a human body because of the rare opportunity to learn and practice the spiritual life. The aspiration is always to develop a mind of compassion and to realize sunyata. Consider the following stanzas by Langri Tangpa Dorje Senge on transforming the mind from selfishness to compassion:

Being determined to accomplish
the highest welfare for all beings,
who [themselves] excel the wish-fulfilling gem,[2]
I shall hold them dear.

When accompanying anyone
I shall view myself as the lowest
of all and in the depth of my heart
shall hold dearly others as supreme.

Examining my continuum throughout
all actions, as soon as an emotional
affliction arises that endangers myself
and others, by facing it I shall strictly avert it.

When others, out of jealousy,
treat me badly with abuse, insults and the like,
I shall accept their hard words
and offer the other the victory.

When someone whom I have assisted
and in whom I have placed great hope
inflicts me with extremely bad harm,
I shall view him as my supreme spiritual friend.

In short, I shall offer benefit and bliss to all mothers
in this actual (life) and in the (future) continuum,
and secretly I shall take upon myself
all of the harms and sufferings of my mothers.

Also, having not defiled all these by the stain
of preconceptions of the eight (worldly) feelings[3]
and by perceiving all phenomena as illusory,
free from attachment, I shall be released from bondage.[4]

These passages emphasize the deep compassion of the Bodhisattva--a being who is willing to take on the suffering of others at his or her own expense. Furthermore, they partly explain why Tibetans sometimes say that the Chinese are among their spiritual teachers. For the Chinese, by torturing and killing monks and nuns, destroying monasteries, and continuing to do all they can to destroy Tibetan nationalism, have given the Tibetan Buddhist practitioner ample opportunity to work with anger, patience and compassion. The secret or trantrayana teachings of Vajrayana are intended to transform ordinary energies, many of which we think of as impure or even fearsome, into what is holy and pure. Tantric practices involve visualizations, mantras, and special techniques, all of which require initiations by a legitimate teacher who has herself or himself received a transmission from a legitimate teacher. The only aspect of these practices that we can discuss without touching upon any secret transmissions is the centrality of the guru.

Guru-yoga plays a central role in trantrayana. The student is to find a teacher whom she can trust and respect as her central teacher, and the teacher, too, needs to assess the potential disciple. Master Asvaghosa's text on Guru-yoga states that:

> In order for the words of honour of neither the Guru nor the disciple to degenerate, there must be a mutual examination beforehand (to determine if each can) brave a Guru-disciple relationship.

> A disciple with sense should not accept as his Guru someone who lacks compassion or who is angersome, vicious or arrogant, possessive, undisciplined or boasts of his knowledge.[5]

Although the requirement to have a teacher may raise concerns in a Westerner, we should remember that we use teachers in our own educational systems from grade school to the most advanced levels of academic and professional studies and, in areas of craftsmanship, we have masters and apprentices. Geshe Dargyey offers a rationale in support of Guru-yoga in addition to the need for initiation and proper training:

> Seeing only good qualities in your Guru, therefore, is the way to develop these qualities yourself. Normally most people are blind to their own shortcomings, while the faults of others shine out clearly. But if you did not possess these same faults yourself, you would be unable to recognise them in others . . . . Likewise, if you can train yourself to see only good qualities and never any faults in your Guru, this positive outlook will come to pervade, amplify and reflect your own state of mind. As everyone has the basis Mahamudra or Buddha-nature within him--the clear,

85

uncontaminated state of pure mind established without any true
independent existence--then if you can see your Guru in terms of
a Buddha, you have the possibility of activating and realising your
own Buddha-nature . . . .[6]

The importance of a guru is essential in Vajrayana. Even if one were to
read the Tantric texts, a full understanding of the practices would be
unavailable to someone who did not have a teacher who had received the
proper initiation.

Vajrayana differs from Theravada in the same ways that Mahayana does.
Vajrayana differs from both Mahayana and Theravada in the trantrayana
teachings: the emphasis on guru-yoga, on initiation, and on practices that
include visualizations and mantras.[7] These techniques aim at the same goal
explicit in Mahayana Buddhism: the realization of the fundamental nature of
reality and the embodiment of compassion.

----

1. Tsongkapa, *The Principal Teachings of Buddhism*, trans. by Geshe Lobsang
Tharchin with Michael Roach (Howell, N.J.: Classics of Middle Asia, 1988), p.
89.

2. A wish-fulfilling gem is a gem that gives its owner all that she wishes.

3.The eight worldly feelings are the feelings occasioned by gain and loss, fame and
disgrace, praise and blame, and pleasure and pain

4.Geshe Rabten and Geshe Ngawang Dhargyey, *Advice from a Spiritual Friend*
(New Delhi: Publications for Wisdom Culture, 1977), pp. 16-17.

5. *The Mahamudra: A Guide to Kagyu Mahamudra and Guru-yoga*, trans. By
Geshe Ngawang Dhargyey (Dharamsala: Library of Tibetan Works and Archives,
1978), p. 166-167.

6. Ibid., p. 160.

7. Tsongkapa, *Tantra in Tibet: The Great Exposition of Secret Mantra*, trans. by
Jeffrey Hopkins (Boston: G. Allen and Unwin, 1977), p. 115.

glossary

Abhidamma–a collection of texts of psychological and philosophical analyses based on the Buddha's teachings; one of the three groups of texts in the Tipitaka

Ajahn--teacher, a title and term of respect for a senior monk in the Thai tradition

akusala–unwholesome, referring both to actions and to the three unwholesome roots of action: greed, hatred and delusion

anapanasati--mindfulness of breathing

anatta--not-self

anicca--impermanent

arahant, arahat (arhant, arahat--Sanskrit)--a "pure one," an enlightened beings, someone who has fulfilled all twelve as pects of the Four Noble truths

asava--cankers, taints, corruptions; the sources of suffering: sense-desire, desiring existence, ignorance, and, in some lists, wrong view; literally the word means "influxes" or "effluents"

bhikku (bhikshu--Sanskrit)--a Buddhist monk

bhikkuni (bhikshuni--Sanskrit)--a Buddhist nun

Brahma-vihara--the four "Divine Abodes," viz., metta, karuna, mudita, upekkha

Buddha--an awakened being, a fully enlightened being, one who has discovered the Dhamma

dana--giving food, clothing, shelter or medicine to monastics

deva--a heavenly being, a celestial being, literally "a shining one"

Dhamma (Dharma--Sanskrit)--the nature of things, the way things are, the unconditioned

dukkha--suffering, unsatisfactoriness, dis-ease

Hinayana--the small (hina) vehicle (yana) of Buddhism, the name given by Mahayana Buddhists to those who practiced what we now call Theravada Buddhism

jhana--mental absorption; the term for the meditative states mentioned in Right Concentration

karuna--compassion

kusala--wholesome, refers both to actions and their root motivations

Mahayana--the greater (Maha) vehicle (yana) of Buddhism

metta--lovingkindness, goodwill

mudita--sympathetic joy

Nibbana (Nirvana--Sanskrit)--release from suffering, liberation, enlightenment; literally, 'to become extinguished'

Nikaya--a collection of suttas; the Nikayas are one of the three texts in the Tipikata

nirodha--cessation

pañña--wisdom

samadhi--concentration

sangha--the community of monks and nuns; as a refuge, persons of spiritual maturation

sila--morality

sunya, sunyata--empty, emptiness

sutta (sutra--Sanskrit)--literally, "thread"; a text containing a teaching of the Buddha or one of his chief disciples

tanha--thirst, craving, desire

Tathagata--"thus come" or "thus gone," one who has arrived at realization, a title of the Buddha

Theravada--teaching (vada) of the Thera (Elders)

Tipitaka (Sanskrit: Tripitaka)--the "Triple Basket" of canonical texts of Theravada Buddhism, containing the Vinaya, the Nikayas, and the Abhidamma

upekkha--equanimity

Vajrayana--the Diamond (vajra) vechicle (yana)

Vinaya--the group of texts containing the rules for monks and nuns, their explanations, and the situations in which the Buddha promogated them; one group in the Tipikata

vipassana--insight into conditioned phenomena, directly seeing them as anicca, dukkha, and anatta; the name of a common form of meditation that often begins with anapanasati